A
CANDLE
FOR MY
MOTHER

A Daughter's Journey Toward Gratitude

Inspired by the Stories of

LORRAINE E. NEWTON

By

PAMELA L. NEWTON

Dear Charles – Life long
friend are so rare and such
a treasure. You are that for
me. Thank you for so many
fun times! Love
Pam

FIRST EDITION

◆

Printed in the United States of America

ISBN: 978-1-7321732-1-7

To my clever, fascinating, and loving sisters

Barbara, Donna, and Kathleen

♦　♦　♦

Mom's greatest gift of all

Contents

CONTENTS

Acknowledgments

There is an old African proverb: "It takes a village to raise a child." In my case, it has taken an entire worldwide community to bring forth this book. There are so many I wish to thank for their relentless efforts, unwavering belief, and constant encouragement. Bravo! to you my beloved community. You have my undying gratitude and heartfelt appreciation.

THE TEAM — Stacey Healey, COO and chief project director; without Stacey I can assure you this book would still be a dream. Nan Sumski, publicist extraordinaire. Clayton Guiltner, producer and editor of our Mom stories. Darrin Luginski, cameraman. Patrick Brown, everything digital. Ana Reina, ideator and events. Matt Dugan, social media partnerships. Kimberly Offenberg, partnerships. Hanna Harrison, photographer. La Manda Davis and Emmanuel Young, interns. The Huntington Beach Central Library. The folks at the Los Angeles Film School: Hal Lieberman, program director; my colleagues C. Michael Brae, Nathan Chitayat, Guy Langvardt, Donna Loyd, Marcus Thomas, Hiram Sims; and especially my students. The relentless pursuit of your dreams gave me the inspiration to pursue mine.

THE EDITORIAL AND PRODUCTION TEAM — Paula Block and Terry Erdmann, who said yes in the beginning; knowing I had them on board gave me the faith that I might not embarrass myself. Lisa Tener, Paul Ruditis and Nancy Pines, invaluable advisers. Stuart Horwitz, story editor. Anne Greenberg, copy editor and guide. Phyllis Ungerleider and Peter Kelly, editors working under impossible deadlines and across the globe. Maria Arellano, proofreader. Maria Villar, book designer. Christopher Alonzo, illustrations.

THE STORYTELLERS — The individuals who so generously shared their Mom stories highlighted online and in the book's marketing campaign. Jasmine Aivaliotis, Brandon Avery, Sanjay Brahmandam, Antoinette Callander, Jonathon Callander, Bill Connolly, Kathleen Dolan, Moriah Garcia, Nicole Henderson, Rachel Henderson, Edward Kelly Jr., Karina Lopez, Donna Loyd, Mary Lou Matthews, Sean McCormack, Gwendolyn Mukes, Kevin Mulhare, Mary Nagy, Canh Nguyen, Regina Palis, Emmy Queliz, Amber Rhabb, Robin Roth, Kevin Santiago, James Simmons, Akello Stone, J.C. Sullivan, Sam Teaford, Rhandy Torres, Patricia Vandermeer, Pete Vandermeer, Tina Vonn, Mekka White, Fleur Zanna, Jose Zepeda, Laura Zhang.

MY FRIENDS — The people we love who make life worth living. There is not room to mention everyone here, so please forgive if your name is not listed. I love and appreciate all who have befriended me in life. You are not forgotten. Elena Cappadona, best friend without equal. Steve Stambaugh, best friend's husband who kept the coffee coming. Kristen Funk, amazing roommate, encourager, and fellow adventurer. Ginny Hill, wise counselor. Brian David Stambaugh, guru godson. Grace Cappadona, Tina Foster, Jose Gullian, Christina Hahni, Andrea Hein, Thomas Jackson, Samantha Kelly, Patrick Nguyen Khac, Hannah Landsborough, MiMi Le Blanc, Terri McKeever, Jon Nees, David Newman, Titus Odedun, Elena Perrotta, Ron Peterson, Harrison Reiner, Kent Sampson, Diane Speigle, Karen Strickholm, Lorraine Turnbull, Bonnie Van Schaick, Ray and Cindy Vernon, Nancy Wagner, Charles Wallace, Tracy Windless, Curtis Wong. All my colleagues at DreamWorks Animation and Paramount Pictures.

MY CHURCH — Pastor Bobby and the friends who surrounded me, spending hours drinking coffee and engaging in great discussions. Louise Dunn, Tricia and Pete Vandermeer, Thelma Rosiak, Richard Hauser, Joe and Cathy Rosenblatt.

MY BOOK CLUB — Teresa and Kevin Cullen, Fred Andresen, Angela Rubio, Barbara June Dodge, Claudia Sawaya, Cora Judd, David Sigler, Dick McDonough and Leslie Arnold, Ernest Cisneros and John Hawkins, Karen Cordova, Nan Roberts, Pamela Edwards, Richard P. McDonough, Theresa and John Hoag, Tom Buchanan, Carole Gelker, Sara Robinson.

MOM'S FRIENDS — Ava Jamieson, Peggy Nees, and Margie Barnes, who provided so much material used in the writing of this book.

MOM'S TEAM — I will never forget Dr. Michael Berman, who gave my sisters and me three more years with our mom. Roger Anderson, who kept her laughing and so much more. Del Lauterback and Nancy Treister, who helped care for her in her final days.

And to the kindness of strangers, my gratitude.

Some Unique Things About This Book

♦ This book contains several blank pages where you can doodle, write, draw — paste in a favorite picture, include a poem, or decorate the page with stickers and sparkles. Here you can personalize this work with your own thoughts and remembrances that come to you as you read the chapters. You can also create special messages to your mom for her to read when you give her this book as a gift (or maybe you'll keep it as your own form of therapy).

♦ My author's website, PamelaLNewton.com, is full of lots of extras. You will be able to listen to some excerpts from the tapes my mother and some of her friends recorded and see photos of our time in Iraq and on our travels. You can read my blog, which chronicles the journey of this book from dream to reality and the marketing campaign we built. The marketing aspect of the website was created so my film school students could see the oft-winding road of a new project and follow along on the adventure.

♦ If you listen to the recordings of the stories, you may notice some differences between what is written and what is spoken. That is because some minor edits were done or corrections made. But most often the differences exist because my mom was still alive when the tapes were transcribed, and she read through and made written corrections. Her spoken versions of the stories don't include those corrections, but the book does. She never re-recorded any of the stories before her death.

♦ Spelling some words Mom spoke on the tapes she recorded were a challenge. Some were written in letters, and some were corrected by her in the transcribed tapes. But they didn't always match. If you have concerns about the spelling of a few words in this book, I can appreciate that. So did I. When in doubt, her corrected spellings were used or those from her letters, which are undoubtedly phonetic.

Preface

Whether it is destiny or chance that delivers us to the parents we inherit, there can be no mistaking the impact a parent has on our life, especially a mom. Some of us are not so fortunate and get the kind that sends us into years of therapy. Others hit the jackpot. But most of us have one that falls someplace in between. Like my mom, imperfect perhaps, but my sisters and I never had any doubt that we were wanted, loved, and held to a higher standard.

Mom became the center of our family when Dad died of cancer when I was only nineteen. Years later, I was in my mid-forties when my mother died. She had been diagnosed with ovarian cancer three years earlier. That gave me some time to grasp her impending departure; even so, I felt cheated by her death. Yet I was much luckier than Mom was. She was only twenty-six when her mother dropped dead of a stroke walking home from lunch with friends in Duluth, Minnesota. Mom was living in Southern California at the time with a three-month-old baby and didn't have the money to go to the funeral. Mom's heartbreak is evident by the teardrops splashed all over the letter from her sister giving the details of their mother's passing and funeral.

I once asked my mom if she missed her mother. She paused and then quietly responded, "I do . . . every day of my life." Now I understand, and I thank her for telling me that, because I don't feel so crazy for missing her every day of my life.

It is strange the journey that loss and grief takes one on. Lighting a candle started as an act of desperation while she was dying, which then transformed into a comfort and a tradition after her death. It became a way to honor my mother while remembering her gifts to my sisters and me. This book is a part of that journey, and I hope you enjoy traveling with me. But more importantly, perhaps this book will inspire you to think about your own mother, your journey together, and all the gifts your mother gave to you.

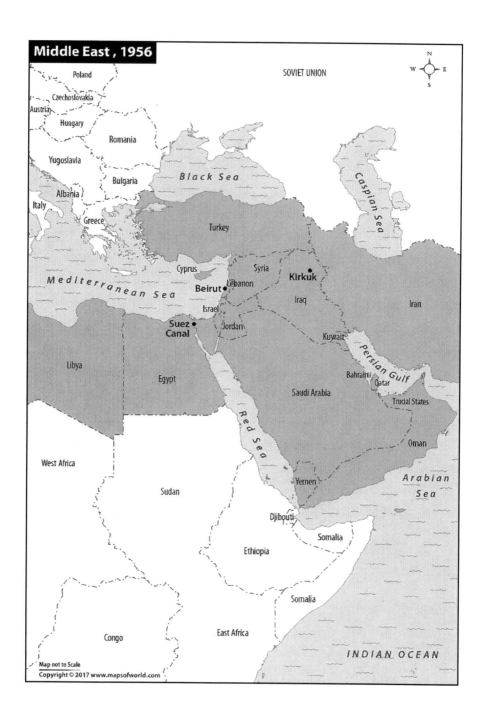

Middle East , 1956

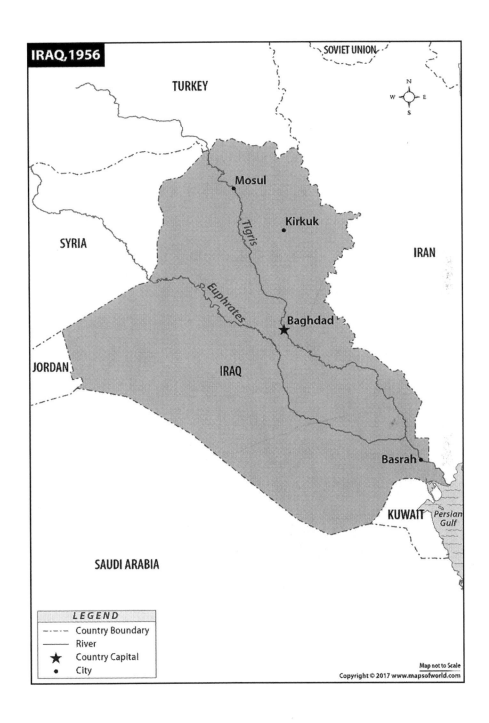

IRAQ, 1956

SOVIET UNION

TURKEY

N
W   E
S

Mosul

Kirkuk

SYRIA

Tigris

IRAN

Euphrates

Baghdad

JORDAN

IRAQ

Basrah

KUWAIT

Persian
Gulf

SAUDI ARABIA

LEGEND
— · — · — Country Boundary
————— River
★ Country Capital
• City

Map not to Scale
Copyright © 2017 www.mapsofworld.com

Imagery © 2018DigitalGlobe. Map date ©2018 Google

CLUBHOUSE

NEWTON HOUSE

Imagery © 2018DigitalGlobe. Map date ©2018 Google

A
CANDLE
FOR MY
MOTHER

Westminster Abbey

Prologue: "I promise"

A by-product of studios creating outstanding entertainment is that the remarkable characters and worlds can be used by product manufacturers as themes for their merchandise — such as *Star Trek* costumes, princess sleeping bags, or any number of toy lines. Many businesses partnered on movie launches to create exciting promotions for their customers, such as McDonald's with its Happy Meal. And entertainment companies are not the only ones who license their characters or images. So do toy companies, artists, bands, sports teams, and corporations, among many others. It is a multibillion-dollar business, and this was my world.

When my mother was first diagnosed with cancer in January 1996, I had been working at Viacom Consumer Products, the licensing group for Paramount Pictures, for six years and was the vice president of Merchandising and Licensing. From my office on the third floor of Paramount Pictures' Marathon office building, one could see the Hollywood sign. It was magical to drive onto the historic studio lot every day and be a part of such a crazy industry. Flying to New York to meet with Tom Cruise about a *Mission: Impossible* interactive game. Or walking over to the television set to talk with the *Star Trek* actors. Or seeing Mel Gibson throw open the double doors at the studio, where he was editing his Academy Award–winning movie, *Braveheart*, and seeing his amazing blue eyes as he greeted my boss and me with, "You must be the licensing ladies," kept me in awe. But I never lost sight of how small in the big scheme of things the licensing and merchandising division's revenue was compared to the revenue generated by movies and television shows. While important, licensing is only a small percentage of a studio's revenue, unless of course you are Disney.

Even though my studio job was intense, I insisted on being the one to go with Mom to the doctor's office that cold January day. Why, I will never know. I am probably the most emotional of my sisters, and we were all worried the news would be bad, as her symptoms were severe. While we were in the waiting area, I kept running to the bathroom to try to pull myself together. Each time, my mother asked if I had a problem. Before too long, we were in the examining room, sitting next to each other in silence, as I did not trust myself to speak. As soon as the doctor walked in the door, I started to cry, and he hadn't even said a word! My mother was very stoic as she faced the news. Obviously, I was not. There it was. The diagnosis: Stage 4C ovarian cancer. Very advanced and she would surely die from it.

Somehow, I got us home. When we walked in the door, I sat down on the sofa, tears streaming down my face, sobbing about how I was losing my best friend, and I just didn't know how I could pull myself together to go into work. Mom sat there quietly for a while as she watched me completely fall apart, finally saying, "But I am the one who has been diagnosed with cancer."

The irony of her statement was completely lost on me as I whole-heartedly agreed with her, "I know. I know. It's so awful." I am horrified to admit that in that moment I gave her no support or hope that this fight could be won, so lost was I in my wretchedness.

It turned out catastrophe was not imminent. When Mom asked the specialist how long she had, Dr. Michael Berman answered, "With treatment, maybe three years." It was time to get busy and figure out how we were going to manage Mom's care. My sister Kathy is a scientist, and we relied on her to oversee the treatment; my sister Donna, as Deedee prefers to be called as an adult, lived close by, so she took Mom to doctor appointments if Mom's friend Del couldn't. Donna and Mom often went out to lunch and swim class. As the businessperson, I took on the role of fighting with the insurance company.

My sisters and I talked about how much care Mom was going to need after her surgery and when she started chemo. Should we look for a twenty-four-hour caregiver? Should I quit my job? What were our options? Then the love of my life, Roger, who was changing careers to write spec scripts and concept television shows said, "I can write from anywhere. Why don't I move in with your mom?" Right then, I decided to accept his proposal made eight years earlier to marry him. If he could find it in his heart to take care of a woman who wasn't even his mother, then surely I could find the courage to marry again. We quietly wed that March, at sunset on a cliff overlooking the Pacific Ocean in Monterey, where I was working on the opening of the Bubba Gump Shrimp Co. Restaurant and Market, based upon Paramount Pictures' *Forrest Gump*.

Mom went in for her first of three major surgeries. Roger gave up his apartment and most of his possessions to move in with Mom, while I kept my little one-bedroom near the studio, commuting to Mom's house on the weekends. It turned out Mom and Roger got along famously, both having a wicked sense of humor. It all worked well for the next two and a half years.

Then, in September 1998, my boss asked me to fly to London to meet with Tim Burton, who was directing Paramount Pictures' *Sleepy Hollow*. The movie was based on the classic story "The Legend of Sleepy Hollow" with its famous character Ichabod Crane (played by actor Johnny Depp) and, of course, the Headless Horseman. Tim is known for dark gothic and fantasy films such as *Beetlejuice*, *Edward Scissorhands*, and the animated musical *The Nightmare Before Christmas*.

Alongside his quirky projects, Tim Burton is wildly successful, having also directed such high-profile films as *Batman*, *Batman Returns*, *Planet of the Apes*, and *Alice in Wonderland*. Given this, we had lofty hopes for creating a strong program of products around *Sleepy Hollow*. The purpose of the trip was to see some of the sets, assess licensable elements, and most importantly, discuss the licensing plans for the movie and hear Tim's thoughts.

Mom was doing okay when I was asked to take this meeting.

She was in her third round of chemo, ambulatory, and still at home with Roger by her side. He had never been to London, so the idea of giving him a break from his 24/7 caregiver role sounded like a good idea. He could do some sightseeing while I attended the meetings. I could extend the trip by a couple of days to give us a chance to go exploring together. It would be for just a week. Donna and Mom's friends would care for her in our absence. With Mom's encouragement, we booked the trip.

In an instant, things changed. A few days before we left, Mom fell coming out of the doctor's office after chemo. Mom hated making a fuss, so she came home insisting she was fine. Shortly afterward, she began to deteriorate — apparently, the fall had triggered something. A couple of days later, Roger called to tell me the paramedics were at the house and an ambulance was taking Mom to the emergency room. I left work in Hollywood, fighting Los Angeles traffic for an hour and a half to arrive just as she was being settled into her hospital room. Later that evening, I found myself standing at her bedside, asking if I should cancel the trip. She would not hear of it. She loved traveling and was delighted when this trip came up, remarking how much she wished she was the one going. But I was still worried. She looked so frail, so helpless. If I was to go, I needed to know she would be all right.

"Mom, please don't die. *Please* don't die while I'm gone, or I will never be able to live with myself," I begged as I held her hand and choked back tears.

"I won't," she replied. "I want you to go."

"Then you must promise me you won't die. Promise?"

"I promise."

Leaving Mom in the hospital felt like abandonment. I thought that what the doctors and nurses would see was "a fat old woman" as she herself put it, now bald from chemo, forced to fight this barbarian at war within her body. How could they see the woman I cherished? The woman who raised me and my three sisters. The woman who gave us a sense of adventure. The woman who bore me and protected me and disciplined me and encouraged me and held me in heartache and in joy. This fierce woman was now endangered, and I was walking out the door. Yes, my sister Donna would be there, but I still could not stop feeling worried sick about my decision. A day later, Roger and I were on a plane to London. I could think of little else than my mom on the flight and during the trip.

My thoughts drifted back to where it all began. Lorraine Ellen was born October 5, 1922, in Duluth, Minnesota. She was such an adventurer and master saleswoman, even from a young age. At fourteen, she convinced the owner of a local drugstore to allow her to demonstrate her dad's essential invention, Bud's Stocking Rinse, the best at preventing runs in ladies' nylon stockings. Nail file in hand, she would slide it up an untreated stocking, causing an instant run. Then she would dip the other stocking in Bud's Stocking Rinse and move the same nail file up the leg with no run in sight. She had a twinkle in her eye when she revealed the secret to me: "It was all in how you held the nail file."

After Mom graduated from high school, she worked for the telephone company. In her early twenties, her father had an opportunity to move to California for work, so she moved with her parents to Long Beach. When her father's job opportunity faded and her mother's first stroke sent her parents back to Duluth, Lorraine stayed in Southern California. She had recently met the man she would marry, Donald Newton. Mom's siblings happily lived their whole lives in the Midwest. But not Lorraine. She was determined to see the world. Leaving Duluth was her first step.

In the mid-1950s, few American families lived overseas. By this time, Mom was married and the mother of four little girls. She had never lost her desire to travel the globe. The only way this would happen now was if my father took a job overseas where we all could join him. I can only imagine how convincing Mom was to have encouraged my homebody father to take an overseas assignment. My father's job as an oil driller, sometimes called roughneck, was to work on derricks rigged to drill for oil. Oil drillers were not paid much in those days, and overseas jobs paid better. Working overseas was different back then, because companies were much more paternalistic with their workers. I like to say that we had a millionaire's life on an oil driller's salary. We lived in unfamiliar places, had a servant, traveled throughout Europe, danced at the company club, and survived a revolution, a hurricane in the Atlantic, and family separations, all with my sisters and me held in the strong arms of our devoted and protective parents. Everything was an adventure to Mom. Even as she faced death, I did not see her afraid. I was afraid, though. I was not my mother's daughter in that regard.

After the meetings with Tim Burton successfully concluded, I found myself desperate to get to a church. I'm not sure what I thought it would accomplish exactly, but at the first opportunity, I suggested we visit one of the most famous sights in London: Westminster Abbey. Roger, thinking I really meant to enter and go exploring for Sir Isaac Newton's tomb along with resting places of lauded kings and poets, began looking around the abbey's magnificent entrance hall in awe. At the same time, I was searching through the crowd for quite a different purpose, a man of the cloth. Riddled with guilt, fear, and grief, I kept thinking I should have canceled the trip. What if Mom died while I was not with her? How could I stop the pain of her looming death?

Then, traversing the nave, a short distance in front of me appeared a rector or a deacon — a clergyman of some kind. He was dressed in black and wore a white collar. That was good enough for me.

I dropped Roger's hand in a mad dash to intercept the striding clergyman, grabbing him with such determination that he stopped instantly and looked at me curiously, his head cocked to one side. Tears flowed as I looked into his questioning eyes. All I could manage was a whisper, and he had to lean forward to hear me, "Will you please pray for my mother? She's dying, and I am not there with her." I could say no more.

We moved to one side of the church with Roger, who had

caught up to us by this time. The rector gently placed a hand on my shoulder saying words I cannot remember, yet in the moment, found most comforting.

Afterward, Roger thanked him, for I still could not speak, and we walked farther into the church. By now, Roger realized that sightseeing was not at the top of my agenda. He waited to see what I would do. Close by was a section with candles. We stopped. I lit one, silently pleading yet again for God to keep my mother alive. And she did survive that trip, living almost three months, not passing until three days after Christmas in 1998. I was so grateful.

Little did I know that at that moment in Westminster Abbey, I had begun a tradition I keep to this day. Whenever I travel and I am able, I visit a church to light a candle for my mother.

For the next six years, life was good. Yes, I missed Mom, but Roger helped to make life fun again. With his newfound freedom, Roger spent his time remodeling our house, writing his stories, and thinking about what he wanted the rest of his life to look like. I continued to work at Paramount Pictures. I did not travel much in this job, but we did take a couple of holidays and extended business trips where I visited a few churches: Sedona, Arizona; Chimayo, New Mexico; Paris, France; Florence, Italy; Monaco. In each, I lit a candle for my mother with no specific thought other than for my solace and as a way to honor her.

Abruptly in the fall of 2004, Paramount Pictures reorganized and closed our division. All but a handful of us lost our jobs. As an executive, I was one of the first to go, effective December 31. I really loved my job, but most of all, I loved my team and the people in our group. They were spectacular. Now, along with Roger, I too was in the position of thinking about what the rest of my life would look like. We shared many laughs, even fantasizing about taking a yearlong cruise to write. But being the practical one, I knew that would have to wait until some financially secure time in the future. Some heavy job hunting lay in front of me.

Without warning, two months after my job ended, the inconceivable happened. Roger died suddenly of a heart attack. He was so young — just turned 55. Now not only was I faced with rethinking my working life but rethinking my personal life as well. How does one survive such loss? All of a sudden, I realized that I was the same age when Roger died as my mother was when my father died. Oh, how I longed to talk with Mom.

Grief is a peculiar companion, demanding more of us at one time versus another. Right then, I felt like grief was a relentless consort, and I struggled rather unsuccessfully to pull free. Dementors from the Harry Potter books, the ones who drain peace, hope, and happiness, leaving an "empty shell," struck me as a likely analogy for the form my grief assumed. It took time. It took going to Africa to do some volunteer work. And it took going back to work again to stabilize the shifting sands of my life.

In May 2006, I received a call from the head of international licensing at DreamWorks Animation, asking if I would be interested in a six-week consulting assignment starting on Monday. I didn't hesitate: "You bet!" Well, six weeks grew into eight months, and that grew into a full-time position, much to my delight.

DreamWorks SKG was cofounded in 1994 by high-powered Hollywood veterans Steven Spielberg, Jeffrey Katzenberg, and David Geffen with a heavy investment by Paul Allen, cofounder of Microsoft. In 2004, the animation studio was spun off into its own publicly traded corporation, DreamWorks Animation SKG (DWA) with Jeffrey Katzenberg as CEO. I went to work for this entity. DWA won the first Academy Award for an animated feature film for *Shrek*. It went on to produce the beloved animated movie series *Madagascar*, *Kung Fu Panda*, and *How to Train Your Dragon*, among others.

I was still involved in the licensing industry as I had been at Paramount Pictures, but now my focus moved from the U.S. to the international side of the business. It was a wonderful occasion to use what I knew and grow my skills globally. Travel was intense, but that was fine with me. In fact, I welcomed it. There was less time to dwell on the loss of Roger, and the job afforded a wonderful opportunity for me to begin anew.

I never felt closer to my mom than when I was traveling, and at DreamWorks I was logging over 100,000 miles a year. These monthly trips provided me the opportunity to reflect on my mother and all that she gave me in this life. Mom's adventurous spirit was with me on every trip, in every country, encouraging me to make the most of each moment. If ever I was tempted to lie in bed some Saturday in Paris, for instance, I could feel her disgust at wasting a chance to go exploring. I simply could *not* stay in bed and would head out of the hotel to see what I could find.

It occurred to me that the path my life was taking was akin to that of my mom's. In the coming pages, you'll see how the traveling that our family did to Iraq and points beyond was an amazing foundation for the journeys of my adult life. The things that happened or that I experienced on my DreamWorks corporate business trips often triggered some remembrance of my mother and my childhood. These memories became the reflections and gratitudes that I expressed in my church visits where I would light a candle for my mother.

No. 195260

Passport photo:
Kathy, Barbara, Pam, Lorraine, Deedee

1 "I'm going to see places, come hell or high water!"

In 1927, oil was struck at Baba Gurgur, just north of Kirkuk, by the Turkish Petroleum Company. For a couple of decades, Baba Gurgur was known as the world's largest oil field. The oil field proved to be extensive and formed the basis for oil production in northern Iraq. The Kirkuk field had over ten billion barrels of proven oil reserves.

The Turkish Petroleum Company was founded by Calouste Gulbenkian, a British entrepreneur of Turkish-Armenian heritage. Turkish Petroleum Company was the predecessor of the Iraq Petroleum Company (IPC). Calouste Gulbenkian held 5 percent of IPC, hence his nickname, Mr. Five Percent, which made him one of the richest men in the world. The other 95 percent of IPC was owned by four of the world's largest oil companies located in the Netherlands, France, the U.K., and the U.S. with 23.75 percent each. IPC had a virtual monopoly on oil exploration and production in Iraq until 1962.

Beginning in the early 1950s, local resentment of foreign control over the oil production of Iraq started gaining momentum. There was a growing Arab nationalism and a sense among many ordinary Iraqis that they were being exploited by the West. These tensions built during the 1950s and 1960s when we were there, resulting in the overthrow of the Iraqi king and, ultimately, the nationalization of IPC.

Meanwhile, Egyptian army colonel Gamal Abdel Nasser led the overthrow of Egypt's monarchy in 1952. In 1956, after the U.S. and the U.K. withdrew their financial support of the Aswan Dam, Egypt nationalized the Suez Canal Company as a way to finance the project. This event caused the Sinai War between Egypt and Israel, France, and the U.K., who wanted to regain Western control of the canal. The Suez Crisis delayed my family's planned departure to Iraq as we were scheduled to go by ship through the Suez Canal.

Nasser's popularity in Egypt and the Arab world escalated after he nationalized the Suez Canal and used his popularity to fan the flames of discord in the Middle East. Calls for pan-Arab unity under Nasser's leadership increased, culminating in the formation of the United Arab Republic between Egypt and Syria in 1958.

This was the bubbling political cauldron of unrest and rebellion my family relocated into when we left California for Iraq in 1956. They were turbulent times. Here begins Lorraine's story.

LORRAINE — LAKEWOOD, CALIFORNIA, 1956

A rogue of sorts, Don Newton looked much like Vincent Price. He was 6'4", blue eyed, and about 185 pounds. Muscular from a life of hard labor, he had a shock of receding brown hair and a nose broken more times than even he could remember from fistfights on the oil rigs to establish his authority. Yet he was the only oil driller I knew who had manicures on a regular basis and loved to dance as much as Fred Astaire. He was eleven years older than me when we married in 1946. I was twenty-three, and Don was thirty-four.

Ten years later, we were the proud parents of four little girls — Barbara, eight; Deedee, seven; Kathy, just turning six; and Pammy, three — and living in the quiet neighborhood of Lakewood, California, a suburban community about thirty miles south of Los Angeles. It was comprised of single-family homes built after World War II to meet the demands of returning GIs armed with their GI loans. This was Don's second assignment in the Middle East. His job in Saudi Arabia didn't work out when the company reneged on their promise to bring us all over.

Now he was working for the Iraq Petroleum Company, and I was poised to realize that grand adventure I'd always wanted. The Middle East was not necessarily what I had in mind, but it would do for a start. For a Midwestern small-town girl, Iraq fit "exotic" to a tee. It conjured up "Ali Baba and the Forty Thieves," markets filled with silks and gold, and travel in Europe on vacations. How could I complain? My wish was about to be granted more heartily than I expected. My fears were small in comparison with the excitement I felt.

After fourteen lonely months apart from my husband, finally, the arrangements had been made. My daughters and I were to depart New York on November 16, 1956, on the passenger ship the SS *Exeter*. The house was sold furnished, the trunks shipped and waiting in New York, bags packed when a telegram arrived from Standard Oil Company: "Urgent, in view of Middle East situation departure deferred. Do not proceed to New York."

A day later, a cablegram from my husband arrived: "Ok here. Mail unreliable. Coming home if trouble reaches us. Reports exaggerated. Love Don."

Reports exaggerated, hardly. Air observers described three major pumping stations on fire near where Don was working. The Sinai War between Israel, the U.K., and Egypt was raging. The Suez Crisis had closed passage through the Suez Canal and with it, our route to Iraq.

I was in a quandary. Should I try to get the house and furniture back permanently? Should I insist Don come home and just forget the whole idea of living overseas? If the move didn't go off as planned, I could console myself with the fact that I wouldn't be held in very high regard over there anyway. Don had written after our fourth daughter, Pam, was born that one of the Arab men on his crew commented, "Oh, it is terrible about your tragedy! Why don't you send your woman back to her parents and go out and buy a new wife to give you big, strong sons?"

I had also been enduring the fears and concerns of

my family and friends for months. "You're going where? WHERE?" "Lorraine, you're crazy taking those four little girls there!" "It's primitive, backward. Why, they don't even speak English." And so the comments went.

It was hard for me to reassure them, for what little I did know would not have made them feel any better. Don led me to believe this place where we were going in the middle of the desert was desolate, devoid of life as we know it. I had no reason to doubt him. I had been enduring his lonesome letters on and off for three years now. I would not know until we were established in camp how inaccurate the reports of my forlorn husband had been.

With the delay, I had no choice but to rent back the furnished house I had just sold. I opened the couple of trunks that remained and waited for the political situation to improve. Christmas loomed. The company said we would not be able to leave until after the New Year. We settled in to make the best of it, while I borrowed back the decorations for the small Christmas tree I had bought. Kathy's birthday arrived on December 17. There was cake and ice cream, balloons, party hats, and presents being opened when the telephone rang.

"Mrs. Newton?"

"Yes."

"Mrs. Newton, this is IPC New York calling. Can you and your daughters be ready to leave the day after tomorrow? We have made arrangements for you to join your husband in Iraq and are holding five tickets at the Los Angeles International Airport TWA ticket counter. The flight departs at 7:00 a.m."

At last, a window of opportunity had opened. It seems the political situation had improved faster than expected. But only thirty-six hours to prepare, with a car to sell, additional trunks to ship, clothes to wash, bags to pack. What the heck — I never said no to anything in my life. "Yes, we will be ready."

Heavens! There was not a moment to lose. I called my close friends for help, and the race was on. Predawn the morning of departure, three cars showed up. One with the backseat removed for the twelve, yes, count them, twelve pieces of luggage, another for all of us, and yet another for our friends. The stage was set for our five-day journey to Iraq.

THE TEMPLE OF THE MORNING SUN, CANCÚN, MEXICO (CHICHÉN ITZÁ)

I too was looking for a window of opportunity to open. For eight months, May to December 2006, I consulted in the international group at DreamWorks Animation. The work was long and hard, with lots of travel, but I loved it. When the assignment came to an end, my boss said she was creating a new position that she would like me to undertake. She asked if I would "hang out" for a while, as the approval for this addition to staff was in process. January passed. Nothing. Then February came and went. Nothing. So what was an unemployed woman-in-waiting supposed to do?

Why, plan a vacation, of course!

I decided to venture close to home, to a resort in Cancún, Mexico. In my research on places to go and things to do near the resort (besides lounge by the pool), I found an important Mayan archaeological site, Chichén Itzá. It is home to a famous pyramid, El Castillo (literally, "the castle"), also known as the Temple of Kukulcán. During the spring and fall equinoxes, the sun shines on the staircases, built at carefully calculated angles, so that the sunlight appears to take the form of the body of an enormous snake joining to its massive carved rock head. Throngs of people come each season to celebrate this marvel of engineering and celestial understanding.

Well, this was fortuitous. It just so happened that my trip was at the time of the March equinox. I read that above the equator, the equinox marks the start of spring, March 20, when night and day are equal, and is celebrated as a time of new beginnings and rebirth. Like my mother, I too was looking for a new adventure, a new beginning, so this seemed like a good omen and a must-do on the sightseeing list.

I was sitting on the plane about to embark on the flight to Cancún when my cell phone rang. It was the job offer. I was to be installed in the newly created position as head of international retail partnerships at DreamWorks Animation (DWA). My role would be to work with the international group's heads of the various regions — EMEA (Europe, Middle East, and Africa), LATAM (Latin America), and Asia Pacific — along with our country agents to develop promotions with retailers. DreamWorks hired agencies in each country or group of countries to conduct licensing and promotional activities and manage day-to-day operations.

My responsibilities included creating ideas for different types of in-store activities, concept sweepstakes that could be run by the retailers, plus seasonal ideas for back-to-school and various holidays. The goal was to build excitement for the store environments where customers shopped while raising awareness of our animated films. Having retailer promotions also helped our licensees and manufacturers sell DWA-themed products into the various retail locations.

All the regional heads were based at the studio except for the head of EMEA. That individual was located in London. It turned out I spent much of my time focused on the European markets working closely with DWA's London team. I built some amazing friendships there and with our various agents. It was a truly creative and collaborative environment in which I thrived.

When I arrived at the resort, I was happy and looked around for a little chapel. I wanted to light a candle for my mother in keeping with the tradition I had started eight years earlier at Westminster Abbey. Lots of weddings took place at this resort but apparently in cabanas on the beach, as there was no chapel. If the beach was reverent enough for a wedding, then it could also function as my church.

One morning shortly after arrival, I wanted to be alone with my thoughts, so I walked to the beach just before sunrise. Being a California girl, I usually went to the beach to watch sunsets. However, I was on the east coast of Mexico, so the dazzling moments on this ocean were the sunrises. I named the little dune I found the Temple of the Morning Sun half in fun and half in honor of the Temple of Kukulcán in Chichén Itzá, where I was soon to visit. I sat, eyes closed, quietly listening to the gentle waves, tasting the salty air, and feeling the cool breeze caress my face. The sun itself had yet to make its appearance, but the wispy clouds reflected the coming light. Such peace.

I gave thanks for my new position, and then I thought of Mom. It seemed my opportunity, like hers, had also begun with a telephone call, and oh, how she would have loved this job! Mom's love of travel and desire to see the world had "infected" us all. In this role, I would be doing just that, and she would be proud of me.

Not all the churches (or sand dunes) I visited offered candles. When that happened, I would sit in quiet contemplation. Or I might do as I did here and "borrow" a candle to mark the occasion. In this instance, it was purloined from the dinner table of the evening before along with some matches secured from the waiter. Because Mom did what she did, all our lives were an adventure too, as we got to tag along. When I lit my candle on the dune, I gave thanks that her fears were indeed small in comparison with her excitement. We were all the richer for it.

Don with Dove plane between Baghdad and Kirkuk

2 "I wouldn't take a million dollars for this trip so far"

Mom, my sisters, and I departed Los Angeles International Airport, experiencing our first airplane flight together. We were not in the air more than a "little while" before Mom began a long letter to her girlfriends back home, chronicling the five days of travel it took to reach Iraq. Her first letters were addressed to all these women together because, as she explained, she would have just written the same thing to each one — there were no copy machines and postage was expensive. Dad complained on more than one occasion about the postage expense of her "excess" correspondence to her friends back home. But he knew she missed them and, I believe, was not really all that bothered in his heart of hearts.

Travel was different in those days. Your tickets were handwritten, envelope-size pages stapled into booklets. Ours would have been a series of pages stapled in each of our booklets because we had multiple flights. Traveling was a huge deal. Los Angeles to New York took about nine hours. The flights were much longer and happened in stages. Today one can fly to the Middle East direct from Los Angeles in about sixteen hours, just about as long as it took to fly over the Atlantic — New York to Copenhagen — in 1956. Besides the amount of time there was the expense. Airplane travel was beyond the reach of the average American.

Flying was a "dress your best" occasion. Men wore suits, ties, and hats, and the women wore dresses and heels. Each Newton daughter had on a little dress, coat, white angora tam, white-lace-trimmed anklet socks with black patent leather Mary Jane shoes, and carried a little purse and a Madame Alexander doll. Mom carried a large bag with our books, coloring books, and supplies, because in those days, there were no in-flight movies, video games, or music to help one pass the time. And as shocking as it may seem today, one could smoke up a storm and drink to excess on flights, and everyone, even economy class, received sumptuous meals served on china with real silverware.

As there were no security checks, it was possible to arrive thirty minutes before departure and still board the flight. You checked in at the desk and walked out of the terminal and onto the plane by climbing a removable stairway. At the bottom and at the top, one was greeted by a beautiful, single, perfectly groomed stewardess. Having to abide by each airline's weight restrictions, all of them were trim. Many airlines gave passengers postcards as they came on board. In writing her letter, my mom did what many travelers did on a plane back then, write.

None of her friends had flown in an airplane, so Mom took great care to give all the details. You can hear the excitement in her words indicated by the many exclamation points found throughout the onionskin pages.

LORRAINE — CALIFORNIA TO IRAQ, 1956

> *Wed. Dec. 19, 1956 10:30 A.M.*
> *Dear Peggy, Phil, Margie, Margaret L., and Catherine C.,*
> *Here I am — only a little while in the air and already writing. Thought I'd give you girls a blow-by-blow description of our trip. I'll mail this to one of you and you can call or send it around.*
> *First off — all of you have been so wonderful to me. I want you to know how very much I appreciate all you did! Without each and every one of you — I just plain couldn't have made this trip! (You all **know** that's true.)*
> *Prescott, Arizona is to our right, the pilot just informed us. Pammy and Deedee are sound asleep. Pam was asleep before we had been in the air 30 min. Barbara and Kathy are coloring.*
> *They have 4 stewardesses on here! This is a beau-*

tiful plane and very comfortable. They just brought us trays for brunch. Did I say "brunch"? Turns out to be 3 thin slices of ham rolled around asparagus spears covered with cheese sauce, toasted English muffins & jelly, fruit salad with dressing, coffee & cigarettes! Delicious! Where's my diet? Haha. Don't worry, I didn't eat it all — but tasted! And the coffee really hit the spot!

We'll be in N.Y. at 4:30 P.M. Calif. Time — 7:30 P.M. N.Y. time. Leave N.Y. at noon tomorrow.

S.A.S. Over the Atlantic — Fri. December 21st 4:30 A.M. European time

I'll go back to the T.W.A. flight. We had filet Mignon + all the trimmings before we landed. Cocktails before dinner, Champagne with it! S.A.S. counter in N.Y. was closed so left my luggage at T.W.A. Took a cab to the hotel. Had the driver go down Park Ave, 5th Ave, & by the big Christmas tree at Rockefeller Plaza. Catherine, I take it all back — the trimmings were out of this world! By the time we all had baths & hair put up, it was after midnight. Got up at 6:30 A.M. and had breakfast in the lovely homey breakfast room at the hotel.

*Got to Standard [Oil] office at 9:00 A.M. Everyone was so nice. They were **amazed** I only had 46 lbs. excess luggage. They gave me expense money & a $250.00 credit slip for the excess baggage from N.Y. to Baghdad. That 46 lbs. cost $238.50!"**

Got a cab at 10:00 A.M. for international airport. I was told it was a 30 min trip. Guess I drew the slowest cab driver in N.Y. We arrived at the airport at 11:35 A.M. with a banged in fender and me a nervous wreck!

---

* $250.00 was a huge amount of money back then, almost a month's wages. The average income of men in 1956 was $3,600 a year, or $300 a month, according to the U.S. Census.

Had to be on the plane at 12:00. Got the fastest redcap in N.Y. & we picked up my 12 pieces of luggage at one end of the airport & ran to the S.A.S. desk at the other end. With 5 people rushing, got my papers in order & luggage weighed and on plane at 12:00!

We were all booked first class, which meant we had sleepers going across the Atlantic. Just like the old Pullmans on trains, beds folded down from the walls with curtains. But nobody wanted to go to sleep. I finally decided we'd all go to bed. I undressed the girls, put them in bed and pretty soon Kathy whispers, "Mommy, I can't sleep. I'm not tired. I can't sleep."

Then everybody else whispers, "Mommy, we can't sleep either." "How can we sleep when we're not tired?" All these little voices.

I kept saying, "SHHHHH." Finally, I said, "I'll tell you what, everybody can get up and we'll get dressed. We'll go sit in the front. BUT everybody has to be quiet because the man back there is asleep." Everyone agreed. Up we got. All dressed. We never laid down again. The only time in my life I had a sleeper going across the Atlantic and I never got a chance to actually sleep in it.

Pam was just too young to sit still and color and listen to stories all the time. She liked to dance and laugh too much. So the stewardesses took her in the galley between first class and tourist and she danced her way across the Atlantic. She never closed her eyes.

While onboard, I continued my letter to my girlfriends.

This is a smaller plane. About 44 passengers. There is only 1 other first-class passenger — an elderly man from Norway who has been so nice. We have 20 seats between the 6 of us! There are 2 stewards and 1 stewardess. All the personnel are Norwegian, they sound so good to me! This elderly man talks just like my Grandpa.

Lunch was about 7 courses with cocktails first. White wine with salad. Red wine with the meat & liqueur with the coffee. The waste of food is awful. No one could eat all they bring! I'm getting tired of looking at food! There's 6 hrs. difference N.Y. & Europe time. After lunch, it was about 9:00 P.M. European time — 3:00 P.M. N.Y. time. They made up the beds, so we had to crawl in! Then they came around and said dinner in 2 hours. I said, "Skip us!" We stayed in bed until 12 P.M. and have been up since. It's now 5:00 A.M. and still only 11:00 P.M. in N.Y.

When we got dressed, they started feeding us again! First, they brought the children bananas, then orange juice. Breakfast was the strangest meal I've ever had. It started with grapefruit, rolls, cheese, milk & coffee. Then 6 kinds of fish and salad! Then veal steak, mushrooms, fried rice, onions, tomatoes, peas! They were so unhappy we didn't eat. We ate the first course and then just looked. You should have seen the girls' faces! Haha. They couldn't have us eat so little & brought in ice cream. The girls ate it. Now they brought in a box of chocolates & they won't take them back. If my kids don't get ill on what they've eaten — they have cast iron stomachs! 30 min and we land in Denmark.

Copenhagen 4:45 P.M. Saturday Dec. 22nd
Took a bus to S.A.S. office when we landed. They got me a hotel room & cab & gave me Denmark money for expenses. The hotel is named Hotel Mercur & is just beautiful. We came right up to bed. I made everyone get up at 11:30 A.M. & they weren't happy. It would be night in N.Y. This

change in time is awfully hard. There is only 6
hours of daylight in Copenhagen now. It was dark
when we crawled in bed at 8:30 A.M. & got dark
again at 3:30 P.M. I sure wouldn't like living here.
S.A.S. called while we were dressing to see if they
could be of service. I said I wanted a sightseeing
tour. They sent tickets right over. We ate lunch at
the hotel & took a cab to the bus for the 1:30 tour
— got back at 4:20 P.M.

When we were leaving the hotel to go sightseeing, the
desk clerks, the manager and the bellhops were all yelling
at our S.A.S. hostess, Marianne, in Danish. I didn't know
what they were saying, but they sure were telling her what
to do. When we got on the bus, I asked what all the fuss was
about and was told the staff all thought the children were
going to freeze and catch cold in this weather as they didn't
have on long stockings. I couldn't see the sense in it since
we were leaving in the morning but relented and bought
each girl a pair.

When we were in the department store, who should we
see but Santa Claus. He was tall and skinny, but it didn't
matter to Pammy. She let out a yip and threw her arms
around his neck crying out, "Santa Claus!" She nearly
knocked him over and caused his beard to go askew. While
she hugged him, he repaired the damage. I noticed all the
clerks were laughing and pointing at Pam. When I inquired
again what the fuss was about, Marianne said, "Well . . .
you see . . . Danish children are not so demonstrative."

To which I replied, "They are just so surprised to see
Santa here." The guide told me he was called Juleman-
den, which translated means "Yule man." So the girls all
learned that in Denmark Santa Claus is called Yule man.
They thought that was quite fun.

After visiting the Little Mermaid sculpture, which looked

quite bleak in the gray frozen harbor, and seeing some additional sights, we returned to the hotel, long socks on, to the approving smiles and clucks of the staff! I picked up my letter again, writing . . .

> *The people here are so nice and friendly, but they don't understand me too well & I sure don't understand them! Had an awful time ordering lunch. Got the girls tomato soup & milk, but the soup had little fish cakes in it. They didn't like them — but, I love them. They were just like my mother used to make. You can't buy them, and I can't explain them. I ordered a famous Danish open sandwich (I thought) & coffee. Got a plate with 2 "different" meats. Haven't any idea what it was but sure didn't like it! There were different pickles and fruits around it. No bread. Hope I do better at dinner. Haha.*
>
> *The tour was very interesting. Would take pages though to tell about it. The girls about froze. It's 5 something above zero. Not freezing, been raining but colder than the girls have ever been in. They are all trimmed for Xmas here. The stores look lovely. They only put plain white lights on green trees. Have seen nothing else on them yet. Tomorrow S.A.S. is to arrange a guide to take me shopping. They even offered a baby sitter for the girls, but I want to take them. I sure hope they remember this! A cab will pick us up at 3:00 P.M. tomorrow for the airport.*
>
> *This has been the most wonderful experience for me. I wouldn't take a million dollars for this trip so far."*

The next morning before the airport, we went shopping. I only bought some Kleenex, nail polish, and a little Danish costumed doll. The plane was an hour late departing. We stopped in Germany, Geneva, and Rome (where it blew a tire that had to be fixed), then on to Damascus, Syria, and finally Baghdad, arriving three and a half hours late. Don was wild. Damascus was terrible. No cameras allowed in the country, they took our passports when we arrived and gave them back when we left. Soldiers all over — dirty, smelly, ugh. I was never so happy to see my American husband waiting for me in Baghdad than I was at the end of that trip.

He stood at the foot of the airplane, surrounded by a four-man welcoming committee from Iraq Petroleum Company. The company was supposed to have notified him of our arrival, but he didn't get that cable until two weeks after we landed. Luckily, I had cabled him, and he got that one. He was way out in the middle of the desert when it was delivered, informing him we would be arriving in Baghdad the next day. Boy, was he on the phone right away to secure a car and driver. Somehow, he made it to Baghdad to meet the plane.

I was taken aback when we looked down from the top of the stairs. Don had been very ill in the months prior to our arrival. He'd lost weight, about thirty pounds, and about half his hair, he had been so sick. Excited, Kathy muscled her way to the front and yelled back at me, "Is that my daddy?"

When Don left to go overseas, I explained to Kathy that her daddy went up in an airplane and that either he would be coming home soon or we would be going where he was in an airplane. I remember being at the Lakewood shopping center when an airplane passed overhead. Kathy pointed her finger to the sky, stomped her foot, and bellowed, "Daddy, Daddy, get out of that plane. Come home, Daddy. You come out of that aeroplane. You come home!"

Well, you can imagine the stares I got. Everyone would turn around and look at this kid and wonder what was up. Some looked very sympathetic and gently shook their heads. I think they thought my husband had died. But Kathy was on a quest to find her daddy. Any man that came to the door, Kathy would sneak around me to point and ask, "Is that my daddy?" I'll never forget when this 4'10" vacuum cleaner salesman knocked, and I answered with Kathy popping out to ask, "Is that my daddy?" She scared the guy half to death, to say nothing of what this was doing to my reputation in the neighborhood.

You can imagine how happy I was when I could finally tell her, "Yes, that's your daddy."

She flew down the steps into his arms. As Don was giving her a hug, she demanded, "Where's my horse?!" You see, Don had promised her a horse. He wasn't a great correspondent, but when he did write the girls, he would use block letters and draw pictures. He told Kathy he was going to get her a horsey when she came. He drew her a picture of one with long ears. She took one look at the picture and said indignantly, "That's no horsey! That's a 'dunkey'!"

I wrote back to Don and said, "Don't think you are going to fool this kid for a minute. She knows the difference between a horse and a donkey. If you think you can get her a donkey, well, she won't have it. She wants a horsey." Instead of going out there and getting a pony (although I never saw a pony in Iraq), he bought a two-year-old stallion for a six-year-old girl and her sisters. We called him Sultan. He was dark brown with a white star on his forehead and white socks. He was beautiful. But you couldn't ride him. He wasn't castrated. All the girls could do was get on his back while the stable boy walked Sultan around in a pen! But Kathy was determined and held Don accountable for the horse he promised her.

By now, we were all crowded around him in frenzied greetings full of elation to have arrived at last. We proceeded to customs, where I whispered, "Don, don't light a cigarette."

"Why not?"

"Because there's a leaky pipe somewhere."

At that he threw his head back and laughed. "No, honey, that's just the smell of the Middle East." I almost died of embarrassment.

We may have arrived in Iraq, but the trip was not over yet. We all piled into three waiting cars and headed to one of the best hotels in Baghdad, the Sandebad Hotel, although I wasn't too impressed with it. It was behind tall iron gates, and the terrace faced the Tigris River that runs through the city center. On the way to the hotel, the girls' eyes were like saucers. We saw women dressed head to toe in black abas and head coverings — hijabs and niqabs. Many of the men were in dishdasha or baggy pants and a variety of head coverings from turbans to keffiyeh (scarves with black braided rope). The landscapes, buildings and transport/carts with donkeys amongst them, was all new. The girls were sure good about everything.

At the hotel, the company welcoming committee invited us to dine in typical Middle Eastern fashion, outside on the patio. I was the only woman there, and the girls were the only children. There, all the men eat out and the women aren't apparent. The girls did discover a new drink, the British beverage called Squash. Lemon Squash became a favorite.

The next day, Don took us on a taxicab tour of the city before we boarded the company's little eight-seater plane called a Dove to take us up to Kirkuk. Finally, we arrived at our new home in Kirkuk town on December 24 at 3:00 P.M., more than five days after the journey in Lakewood, California began. I was ready to start our adventure because to me, this was a great adventure, to be living in a foreign country.

ST. SAVIOUR'S, ST. GEORGE'S SQUARE, PIMLICO, LONDON

I'm a little bit like my mom when preparing for a trip. Of course, she was working to shut down our life in the U.S. and reopen it halfway across the globe, so perhaps not a fair comparison. I was simply going away for a week or two. No matter what, I always seemed to be up most nights before departure putting the finishing touches on my presentations, answering last-minute emails, organizing my out-of-control office (how could it possibly get so messy in just two or three short weeks of residency?). Finally, at three or four in the morning, I'd head home to wash clothes, pack, and be ready for the car that would take me to the airport at 5:00 p.m. that day.

A lovely part of traveling internationally for most corporations is that you fly business class. In my DreamWorks role, where I was on the road almost every month, anything less than business class would have made the work untenable. Because of my lack of sleep and the amount of time I spent on the job, I couldn't wait to get on the plane. Twelve hours with no email, a good dinner with an ice cream sundae (the only reason I stayed awake to eat), and then welcomed sleep. Next thing you know, I would be up, eating a light breakfast, and landing in London. It never felt like I had just traveled 5,437 miles. It felt so ordinary, yet wondrous all at the same time.

Amazingly, Mom never called travel a slog. It was always an adventure. Anytime any of us went traveling she would ask, "How was your adventure?" She didn't complain about the effort required even in modern times. She remained thrilled all her life. I believe the wonder of travel for me is a direct result of my mother's love of travel.

So here I was on my flight, marveling that I could fall asleep in one city and wake up the next "morning" in another so far away. The plane landed at Heathrow on Sunday at 2:25 p.m. I cleared customs, caught a cab to my hotel to drop off my luggage, had a quick shower, and changed for dinner with a friend. I was headed for a pub just up the road from Pimlico tube station. As I came up from the underground, I saw the spire of a petite gothic church on the edge of St. George's Square, just beyond the pub. I was early, so I walked past my destination and over to the church, St. Saviour's. I thought I had stumbled on a little local church and did not realize until I did a bit of research that it had some interesting bits in its background.

According to the church website, the father of famous British actor Sir Laurence Olivier was a curate at St. Saviour's, and Lord Olivier was a choirboy and boat boy (one who carries a little metal "boat" filled with incense). There were other famous folks who worshipped there, but the connection I found most interesting was Diana, Princess of Wales. This was the location where she worked as a kindergarten assistant the year prior to her marriage to Prince Charles. Following the tragic death of the princess, a commemorative tree was planted in the church hall courtyard, and a bench in her memory stands by the main doors to the building.

I wish I had known that when I popped in to light a candle for my mom. I would have sat on the bench and spent a few minutes in appreciation of Princess Diana as well — for the light and kindness she brought into the world. She too was a strong woman like my mom and an adventurer. She wanted her sons to experience ordinary things, while my mom wanted her daughters to experience extraordinary things. The last thing either of them would have wanted, I believe, was for their children to stay cloistered in their respective worlds and not participate fully in life.

But I did not know that when I entered the church. Nor did I know that my world would intersect with Princess Diana's again during the *Kung Fu Panda* concert at Althorp, Princess Diana's childhood home. There I would get my chance to sit under a portico on a bench dedicated to her by the estate staff on the shores of the lake where she is interred. This late afternoon, I knew none of that. I simply crossed the threshold of the church, proceeded to the candles, dropped in some coins, found just the candle I wanted to light, and gave thanks.

My mother took me on my very first adventure. Every time I've touched down somewhere since then, I've felt that same sense of possibility and excitement my mother must have felt during her travels. I realized again what a valuable gift she gave me, paraphrasing her refrain: "This has been the most wonderful experience for me. I wouldn't take a million dollars for this *job* so far."

Club in background with pool and diving board
Life revolved around the club

3 "Boy, this is the life"

LORRAINE — KIRKUK, IRAQ, 1956/1957

We got to our house in Kirkuk town, and it was an enormous structure. Realizing it would be Christmas Eve, Don had given the key to a couple of American women and asked if they would put some food in the refrigerator for us. What a shock when I opened that refrigerator and saw the biggest hunk of raw meat I'd ever seen. Lying on the shelf next to it was a huge head of cabbage with other things that didn't look like anything I had ever cooked with. I had no idea what I was going to do with it all. Not only that, these "friends" had also taken the new linens the company issued and replaced them with used ones and took the only working heater.

It was so cold in that big house. It gets cold in northern Iraq in the winter, believe me. I wanted to bathe the girls that night, but there were no plugs in the bathroom, no heaters. The portable space heater in the living room wasn't working, and I was looking around, trying to figure out what to do when, within an hour of our arrival, the doorbell rang. Two men from the main company camp at Baba Gurgur were at the door. One was a gentleman by the name of Mr. Myers, who invited our family to his house for Christmas Day. I said, "Oh, but we have four little girls. We really couldn't."

To which Mr. Myers replied, "That's why we are inviting you. We have two girls, but they are grown now, and they are back in California. We'd be delighted to have four little girls around." I gratefully accepted, thankful not to have to try to figure out how to cook that mess I had waiting in the refrigerator.

About that time, the man next door came home from work and over to our house to introduce himself. He was Vern Clayton, and his wife was back in the States having heart surgery. When he found out we had no heat, he yelled to his houseboy, "Abdullah, bring every heater we've got in the house over here!" Abdullah managed to find five so we could get a little of the chill off. As there were no outlets in the bathroom, I connected one heater in the bedroom. Then I bathed the girls in the cold bathroom, and we huddled around the warm heater to dry off, put on their pajamas, and climbed into bed.

The next day was Christmas Day. It dawned bright, frosty, and early. I was excited to go into the main company camp for the first time. The house the Myerses lived in was lovely. I fell in love with that house. I realized later it was the only house in camp that had coverings on the divan and chairs that matched the drapes. The Myerses prepared a delicious dinner and had included us with their group of friends. The girls were just angels. It was a wonderful day. You know, there are some remarkably kind and helpful people in the world.

Our house was in a miniature encampment in Kirkuk town, quite a distance from the main camp, where all the amenities were located — like the club house, cinema, library, and pool. Baba Gurgur camp resembled a proper little town with a church, graveyard, school, and lots of single-family houses on tree-lined streets. But I had yet to discover all these wonders.

Our house in Kirkuk town was all I knew at this point, and I wrote, in great detail, about it to my friends.

There are 6 houses alike in this camp kind of arranged in a circle with a high brick wall around them

— iron gates to each house & driveway. In the middle, is kind of a center courtyard with grass, flowerbeds, stone walks surrounding a pond. Three gardeners work the yards with tools the size of tablespoons. They wear turbans and stop to pray about five times a day. Sure seems strange to look out my window on that. There are guards on duty day & night.

It took two yrs. to build these houses by hand! There is a lovely fireplace in each living room, but when they tried them, they didn't work — so they bricked them up! The houses are huge. Downstairs is a big living room (bigger than the one in apt. 3 on 12th St.), big dining room, an English style kitchen — comprised of two rooms with two pantries, bathrooms have wash basin in one room, toilet in another, two big storage closets (each as big as the kitchen in our Lakewood house), long hall & entrance hall, and closet. Up the stairs to two huge bedrooms, one smaller bedroom, two big baths — each has tub, one has shower, and outside the hall is a big porch with clothes lines. Up more stairs to a huge sundeck. Oh, and Asa, our houseboy, has a room & private bath outside the kitchen.

You never saw so much wasted space in your life! The house is all concrete with cement tile floors. The ceilings are all about 12 feet high with a fan in the center of each that looks like an airplane propeller. The windows all open towards the inside with bars and screens on every one. There is a front door, back door & door out of the dining room downstairs. Upstairs one goes off the hall to the porch. It would kill any one of us to try & keep this place up. You have to have a houseboy.

Boy, this is the life — no beds to make — no house to clean — no dishes. I do my own cooking. Feel I can cook cheaper this way.

Every morning, we press a button & Asa brings a tray right up with tea. We prop up in bed and jabber away drinking tea! Haha. When I get to the kitchen, the coffee is made, stove heated, table set, & everything laid out he feels I might need to make breakfast. Then he stands by to help. He also serves.

I could get spoiled very fast. Just told Asa to go rest. He's not used to such nice treatment. He says, "No, Memsaab, Asa work." I told him everything was done. Every time I put a cigarette out, he empties and cleans the ashtray. I can't get used to him. Have to buy him some clothes. He has a brown shirt and pants held up by rope. Will get him a razor too. He looks rough, but sure tries to please. He doesn't want me to do a thing. He's about 25 yrs. old and has a boy 5, girl 3 & boy 5 mo. But think he's only worked for the English & they treat them like slaves. Also he's slow. Also he doesn't speak English well. He can't understand me nor me him.

You should hear Asa & I talk! I use my hands, arms and facial expressions mostly. Wish I could find a good one who spoke more English. He hates to run the vacuum — don't know why. Would rather get down on his knees and sweep it with a brush.

I'm 'mem-saab'. Don is 'sahb' and the girls are 'chikos'.

Had company for dinner last night and asked him to bring the vinegar to the table in the fancy little bottle from the cupboard. In he comes beaming with a bottle of vanilla! One day I wanted a piece of rope & got a light bulb. It's quite an experience! But we make out fine.

He's crazy about Pam but says small chiko — much trouble. Abdullah, the cook/houseboy next door at the Clayton's is her special friend tho. Abdullah wears a turban — has 5 children in Basrah.

He's real good to me. Been with the Clayton's for 8 years so I can understand him pretty well. Anytime I'm baking or cooking he comes over — he takes the spoon out of my hand and finishes.

There are no stores such as we know. I shop for vegs, fruits, meats at the souk (native bazaar). You hire a boy to carry these straw shopping baskets (there are no bags although they sometimes use cement sacks). You buy by kilos and pay with Dinars and fils. The stuff is all outside — the meat hangs from a nail and I just point at what I want & a native just hacks it off with a big knife & hands it to me. I throw it in a basket on top of the vegs, ugh! Then I come home & wash & wash & wash them.

Flour and sugar — they scoop by hand into very thin bags. Then you come home you must sift the flour through a stocking to get out the weevils. The sugar is so coarse, we have to roll it with a rolling pin or else your cakes won't turn out right. I buy eggs 100 at a time. You can crack a dozen to get two good ones. Rice, raisins and nuts — you pick over every kernel for stones, stems, etc. No pork at all is sold here. All meat is fresh — no aging & it sure tastes different. Life here at its best is a challenge.

THE EUROSTAR, PARIS TO LONDON

Hearing Mom's many stories about cooking certainly made me appreciate all the creature comforts of today's modern life in the Western world. She spent so much time on food buying, preparation, and new recipes, she had little time for the housework managed by the houseboy. Having help really was a necessity, even though Mom thought of it as a bit of a luxury. She loved having her tea or coffee served to her on a silver tray in the morning before her day began. It was a little luxury that pleased her so. I may not have had a houseboy, but I did have room service (my fave). I appreciated the luxury of hotel room service. It was my quiet moment before the day began.

On one of my trips to Paris, after a busy day of meetings, I boarded the Eurostar to London. As the train hurtled along at 186 miles per hour toward its destination, I loved looking out at the neat farms, stone villages with their ever-present church spires, and fields surrounded by tall, narrow trees like the ones in Monet paintings. When it was light out, I found it hard to write the updates of the day's meetings my boss was expecting. The views captivated me so. I wondered what life was like in the many towns we passed and became lost in my daydreams.

This late afternoon when my dinner arrived, I was thinking about what life was like for Mom, how different hers was from mine. My mind had drifted back to her many stories about food — the procuring of it, the preparing of it, and the desire to think of something new and different to serve. By contrast, how easy it was for me to find interesting cuisine, both on the road and at home.

I may not have been in a church this time, but I was ever so grateful for how hard my mom worked, especially in this regard. As I was thinking about that, I became hyper-aware of the waiter on the train, the chefs in the kitchen, the dish washers . . . just looking out of my window, there were fields full of crops and animals. I had soared above the countryside seeing banana growers in the Caribbean, coffee bean harvesters in Colombia, and spice sellers in India. It struck me that food now was available with such ease thanks to the packers and shippers, the supermarkets and restaurateurs. In that moment, I had an absurd desire to hug the waiter when he came to remove my tray. But as he was French, I was pretty sure that would not have gone over well. Even when we came back to the States, Mom cooked most of our meals. So I can say with heartfelt gratitude, as one who rarely cooks anything, thank you, Mom (and all food purveyors), for the thousands and thousands of meals you prepared day after day after day.

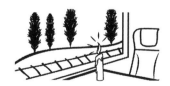

✈

Lorraine with one of the workers

4 "This place and its people are so hard to describe"

LORRAINE — KIRKUK, 1956/1957

I have so many stories of events and activities I found unusual. These are just a few. Kirkuk town was really just a small village back then. The people, unless they worked for IPC or had their own businesses, lived in mud huts, no electricity. When we arrived, I enjoyed going up on the roof to watch life go on around us.

In the mornings, I would see these ladies out in the desert squatting down. I didn't know what they were doing, then finally realized they were going to the bathroom. They didn't have any toilet paper; they used sand to dry themselves and that always made me itch.*

The gardeners at the compound would stop work five times a day to pray to Allah. Each had a little prayer rug. They washed their hands and their face before they began. They would lay out their mats facing Mecca, then kneel down arms out, head bowed to the ground to do their devotions. I would hide behind the curtain and watch. I couldn't take a picture of this although I sure would have liked to. Picture taking was government restricted.

It was hard to believe that they were so far behind the times. They lived in mud huts, few had shoes, women were nothing — man was superior. And how the women worked! They carried five-gallon cans on their heads in perfect balance. The women washed clothes by beating them with a stick in mud!

....

* Each time Mom recounted this story, she wiggled a bit in her chair.

The streets were swept with a straw broom, and roads were built by hand. It took twelve men to do a one-man job. Some tiles were loose in one bathroom. It took three men seven days to repair them. Their only tool was a small clay bowl. They mixed the cement by hand and applied it by hand.

In my house in Kirkuk town, there was a crooked lamp shade that I could not straighten. I told Don. He didn't have any screwdrivers or tools there, explaining the company will take care of it: "You just call the commissary and they'll send someone out to fix it." So I did.

The next day, a big one or two-ton truck (I'd have to see a picture to tell you what size it actually was) arrived. Out of this truck came three men — the driver, the man sitting next to him, and the man sitting in back. They lined up in order. The head man came in first, then the driver, then the man in back third. I took them to show them what was wrong and said, "All you have to do is tighten the screw up there on top."

Having assessed the situation, they all turned around in order and went out to the truck to get the right tool, a screwdriver. Back in they came again in the same lineup with the third man carrying the screwdriver. When they got to the lamp, the third man handed the screwdriver to the second man, who handed it to the first man. He turned the screw and made the lamp shade stay level. I thanked them as they exited in order, got in the truck, and drove away.

Another interesting case was brought to light by the horse Don had purchased for Kathy. Sultan was boarded at the local stable. Old Ollie and his son, Young Ollie, took care of Sultan. When we visited our horse, we were always invited for tea with Old Ollie and his wife, who would fix the chai that was served in little glasses. (Oh, God, the tea was so sweet. I hated it and only drank it to be polite.) I learned quickly to turn my glass upside down or it would keep getting refilled.

One day, we heard a story in camp that I couldn't believe. Old Ollie had a daughter who was fifteen or sixteen years old. Somebody reported to him that she was talking to boys on the street corner. Dishonoring the family just was *not* allowed. At the dinner table, he confronted her and apparently got nowhere on the matter. He whipped out his knife and cut off her head. Killing his daughter was allowed. There were no illegitimate children in the Middle East when I was there. If a girl misbehaved, if she got pregnant, her father would kill her. If her father didn't, her brothers would. If her brothers didn't, then her uncle would or her cousin, but she would be dead. I just couldn't fathom such a thing.

There were just so many interesting customs that we encountered, but this one would have been my undoing. Don was very well-liked by all the Iraqis with whom he worked. One night, we were invited to a party at an Iraqi house. It was a large party, and we were the only foreigners there. The host had pit-cooked a whole lamb that held a chicken that held an egg inside. It was also stuffed with rice. I'd like to note that it was the best meal I have ever tasted in my life. Before we began eating, the host rose and made a speech naming Don as the honored guest. He then reached over, stuck his thumb in the lamb's eye socket and gouged it out. Handing it to Don, he proclaimed, "As our honored guest, you get the eye of the lamb." I almost died, but Don took it, ate it, and everybody cheered and toasted him. I think our host thought he would throw Don with this next move. He gouged out the other eye, proclaiming, "You are doubly honored as our guest." He handed the eye to Don, and by God, if Don didn't eat that one too.

As soon as I could get to him, I asked, "How did you do that?"

"I pretended it was an oyster and swallowed it whole." I could never have done that. I would have been disgraced.

Another time, Don remarked with amazement at how

we Americans, in our efforts to help, often managed to accomplish nothing. When plowing their fields, the Iraqis would use a single wooden plow stick. We stepped in and gave them tractors so more could be done. When the tractors broke down, they just sat there and rusted because nobody knew how to fix them. Another thing, if the equipment used gas, who had the money to buy it? It used to make Don so mad. "I just don't know why we didn't come over here and teach them to be more productive by showing them how to hoe an additional two, three, or four rows at a time with a stick, rather than bring over this expensive equipment."

Then there was a time that Don was out with his driver (all the men had drivers) and needed water. It was the desert. The men carried five-gallon water cans with them at all times. His driver said, "My village is near here. I'll take you there to stop for water." And then he added proudly, "Oh, America give us very good well. We have wonderful water at the village." Upon arrival, he showed Don this wonderful well that the Americans had drilled for them. Then he walked over to another well and dropped a pail down with a rope.

Don questioned, "Why don't we get water from that good American well?"

"Oh, Sahb, no petrol run the motor. We got no petrol here." So it was useless to them. It is amazing how we do things like this in countries that we are trying to help. Ludicrous really.

One class of people could be so cruel to the next class that I couldn't believe it. And dogs — I never saw any cats — the dogs they would kick. If you looked at them when they kicked a dog, they would go after it and kick it harder.

The harsh treatment extended beyond the dogs. The donkeys would be loaded down with stuff on their backs, and they would have a stick and they would hit their hind end, or worse, to make it go faster. What the donkeys didn't carry, the women did. They would carry tremendous loads on their heads with the straightest back and legs. I don't think they would have dared bend a knee or they might have toppled over. It used to gripe me to see a woman loaded down with stuff going down the road with her husband waltzing ahead of her with a walking stick. He was just walking. He didn't have one thing to carry. Ah, but those ladies had gold — gold on their ankles, gold on their arms, gold in their ears, gold in their nose. That was a woman's wealth. Necessary because all a man had to do was say, "I divorce you, I divorce you, I divorce you," three times facing Mecca, and the woman was sent back to her family.

I could never understand the American and British girls who had never read the Koran (the Muslim holy book), yet married Iraqis. I got ahold of two English versions when I first arrived, reading them cover to cover. I felt that as a guest in their country, I should know what was wrong or right to do.

I had tea one morning with some ladies with Iraqi husbands and was horrified to hear them say they hadn't ever read the Koran. These women had babies and had no idea that if their husbands divorced them, those babies belonged to the husband, not to the wife. Furthermore, if their husband died, the brother could take them as a wife.

Another thing I noticed after we'd been there a while was that there were a couple of triangles going on. Married men whose wives were not with them were called "married bachelors." The absence of their wives for such a long time led to some interesting liaisons. I didn't have much sympathy for the wives, though, because some of them would come out for the summer from England, step off the plane, and four days later when the plane went back, they were on it. They wouldn't even stay and give it a go. I always believed that if your husband felt he was doing the best for you, you should stick it out with him. And it wasn't that bad if you looked at the good side. Yes, it was hot! Yes, it took longer to cook.

Yes, you didn't have things the way you had them at home, but what a wonderful adventure it could be.

NOTRE-DAME CATHEDRAL, PARIS

I am always surprised at how little cultural guidance some companies offer to their employees (and their families) who are going to work abroad. While I lived and traveled extensively overseas in my youth, international business experience and knowing the appropriate business etiquette was quite another matter. I was never offered any classes, nor did I think to ask. I thought I was pretty knowledgeable. Of course, I had some sensitivity from all my experiences, but now that I teach international business, I look back and realize some of the mistakes I made.

I was once in a Paris metro station with one of our French agents. Much to my disappointment, we didn't get along very well. When I asked why there were so many barriers at the station, she explained, "The French are not like the Germans, who will pay even if no one is there, so the officials must take measures."

Hoping this might be a tiny point of connection, I joked, before thinking it through, "Oh, a little lawless, just like us Americans."

To which she snapped crisply in her beautifully accented English, "We are nothing like you Americans!" Silly me.

Later during that trip, I participated in a very well-attended meeting at the headquarters of the country's largest retailer. I was responsible for providing a brief DreamWorks overview, and then the managing director of our agency, Marina, completed the rest of the presentation in French. At the end, there was a discussion about the possibilities, and I picked up on some of the promotional ideas that appeared to be of interest and a few next steps, but my normal meeting close would have been to do a recap, just to be clear. Very American of me. Suddenly, a company exec announced as he rose, "*Et voilà!*" and everyone in the room started to disperse.

I leaned over to Marina and said quietly, "There it is . . . what?"

She whispered back, "I'll explain in the car." It seems everyone in the room knew what had been decided — except me. In certain parts of the world, such as southern Europe, the Middle East, and Asia, it can really be helpful to have a native speaker with you in meetings. So much of the communications are nonverbal, inferred. As a direct American, I found Germany and the U.K. shared a much more similar business style, but even there, there were distinct differences.

One of the best things I learned from my mother was to watch what people are doing and then follow suit. She recommended, "If you don't know which utensil to use, look at the rest of the table and follow their lead." "If you don't understand something, be quiet, and when you can, ask a trusted friend." "Speak slowly and try not to use slang." "Be careful about making jokes. Humor doesn't travel well, and worse, they may think you are laughing at them." And so much more.

This particular trip to France, I'd had a couple of cultural awakenings. It would have been fun to talk with Mom and hear her take. I was due to fly home on Friday but decided to extend my trip until Sunday. A definite Mom thing to do. That way, I could gain a bit more understanding and explore some of Paris with my friend Samantha, who joined me from London. After my morning meeting ended, we went to a small bistro for a late lunch that included some inexpensive red wine. The wine was amazing. We commented to the waiter on how wonderful the wine was, unlike what we found at home, and he proudly revealed, "We save the best for drinking in France, and that is why you do not find this in America."

Afterward, Sam wanted me to experience another treat, to taste the flavors of a famous ice cream shop near Notre-Dame. It was the perfect opportunity to pop in to light a candle for my mom. I was fresh from my extraordinary cultural learnings, and thoughts of her were on my mind. As I lit my candle, my gratitude was for her ever-so-practical advice. Mom was a powerful observer, and her recommendations for what to do when you don't know what to do have been invaluable. Thanks, Mom, for teaching me to first watch and listen.

Jon, Peggy, and David Nees

5 "Would you ladies mind if I joined you?"

LORRAINE — KIRKUK, 1956/1957

The day after Christmas, Don got a car and drove me around Kirkuk, which was just a little village back then. He showed me the grocery store, the only department-type store, and the souk, the open-air market full of vendor stalls much like you see today on the travelogues. While he was at work the following week, I had to go in and find some groceries. I took all the girls with me. When I walked into the department store, the owner greeted me with, "Hello, Memsaab Newton. Welcome to Iraq."

"How does he know my name?" I thought. Word certainly got around over there — you didn't need a newspaper. Who else had four little girls? Not one soul in that camp. After the department store and the grocery store, I thought, well, I need some fresh things, so I decided to give the souk a try. I had a car and chauffeur. I instructed him to take us down there. When I got out in the souk with three little blonde girls and one little dark-haired girl, people started coming. They wanted to touch my daughters' hair because they hadn't seen many blondes around and certainly not in the souk. A policeman came by, using his whip to get people to back away from us. "Oh boy," I thought, "I'll have to do this on my own," and left.

I didn't know anyone in town that would go with me. So I waited until the older girls were in school. Then I made the attempt on my own, but it was frightening to me because I couldn't speak the language, and oh, my God, there were flies over everything. But I got used to it, thinking of it as yet another adventure. In fact, I became quite good friends with many of the purveyors, always smoking a Ghazi cigarette with the butcher before we conducted our business.

Don returned to work. He was working about two hours away, so sometimes he would be gone for five days and then home for his days off. I was really looking forward to going to the New Year's Eve party and meeting some of the other wives. Being in town and not in camp was very isolating. But when New Year's morning dawned, the ambulance was at our front door. Don was sick again. He had just recovered from yellow fever when we arrived and could have been experiencing a relapse.

Don called from the hospital and told me how we could come for a visit by taking a bus to camp, then once there, catching one of the camp taxis to the hospital. It turned out to be a two-hour journey with all of us arriving in the early afternoon. I found out later visiting hours were supposed to be 6:00 p.m. to 7:00 p.m., but they let me see him because I had all these children. When we were leaving, Don suggested, "Now, why don't you stop at the club. There's a little dining room in the back on the right. Go in and have something to eat, and then get the bus back to Kirkuk town. That way you won't have to bother cooking tonight." That sounded like a plan to me, so he explained the money and "stuff." When we arrived in the dining room, it was a bit early for the dinner crowd. There was only one other couple, who had just finished their meal. I ordered for the girls, and this woman got up and came over.

"Are you Mrs. Newton by chance? Don Newton's wife?"

"Yes, I am."

"Where's Don?"

"He's in the hospital again."

"Well," she continued, "my husband said when you came in that you had to be Mrs. Newton. I said, no, he was wrong, and he said, who else has four little girls? Nobody but Don. Do you mind if we bring our coffee over?"

"Oh, no, please do." I was lonesome to talk with somebody.

This lovely couple turned out to be Bobby and Ava Jamieson. Bobby was a Scotsman who was quite a kidder. He'd met Aghavni, called Ava by all us Westerners, at the home of Ava's sister and was smitten. Aghavni, whose name means "dove" in Armenian, was an Iraqi, born in Baghdad, from a large Christian Armenian family of nine children.

Ava and Bobby were horrified to find out how we had gotten to the hospital and that we still had to catch the bus back to Kirkuk town that night. Bobby insisted in his thick Scottish brogue, "You're not going on that bus, girl. I've got a car. I'll take you down to town."

Then Ava asked, "Are you going to see Don tomorrow?"

"Yes."

"Well, you're not taking these children. What you do is get the bus up to my house" — and she told me where they lived — "I'll have the children to tea while you go and see Don. Then you come back to have a meal with us, and Bobby will take you all home." The next day went to plan. I thought it was awfully nice of them to take such good care of us. We became lifelong friends after that.

Not all my friendships came so easily. Some took a bit more, shall we say, finessing. One of the British wives had gone to Sadler's Wells Ballet School in London, performed in the ballet there, and started a dance class for the little ones, preschoolers, up at the club. While the older girls were in school on Saturdays, I would take Pam into camp on the bus to participate. There was a whole table of English gals who sat together each week. The club manager would come over to them, chat for a little while, then go and bring them tea and little cakes. I found a small table where I would sit to wait for Pam all by myself. Nobody came and spoke to me, nobody said anything as I sat there week in and week out. I kept telling Don, "I'm going to do something about this."

"What are you going to do?"

"Well, I'm going to watch and see who the ringleader is, and then I'm going to go over and invite myself."

Don said, "Oh, I don't know if you should do that."

"Well, I tell you, I'm going to. I'm not going up there and sit by myself every week while they are having a good time over there!"

About the fourth week, I walked in, determined that to-day was going to be the day. I put Pam down in her dance class, then walked over to the table. "Hi, I'm Lorraine Newton. Would you ladies mind if I joined you?"

A look of shock went around the table and then came "Oh, no, by all means, do."

They introduced themselves and then explained that they all pitched in on the tea and cakes. Fine. I threw in my 100 fils too and sat there and had tea with them. So that's how I got to know them. A couple of weeks after I started this, I no-ticed a lady come in, and she put a little boy into the dance group. She too sat there all by herself. After two weeks, I asked who she was. Nobody knew. So I went over and intro-duced myself and asked her to join us, which she did.

Her name was Peggy Nees, and she was a former Aus-tralian Army nurse married to a Texan that she had met in the oil fields of Kuwait. Peggy and her husband, Mann, and their two little boys, David and Jon, lived in another com-pany camp, Camp 8. She had quite a trek coming into the club with her little boy, Jon, to go to dance school. Her other son would meet her at the club after school and then wait for Mann to pick them up and take them back to Camp 8. Through this chance meeting, Peggy too became a trea-sured lifelong friend.

When dance class ended, it coincided with the time school let out and the workers were returning home. No cars or buses were available to take us back to Kirkuk, so Pammy and I waited at the club for about an hour for the rush to subside. One day, the leader of the group, Maureen, inquired, "How do you get back to Kirkuk?" I explained we took a bus but had to wait about an hour for the schoolchildren and men to get home. Then Maureen suggested, "Why don't you send a note to the school next week and have the girls dropped off at my house? I'm just down the road from here. I'll have you and the girls to tea, then Don can come and pick you all up after work." Maureen had a little boy, Richard, a year older than Pam, and a girl, Julie, around the same age, who became Pam's friends and playmates. Don would stop by after work, have a drink, and then take us home. This lasted for several months until we moved into camp. I was very grateful to Maureen, and she too became a great friend.

After we moved into camp, Maureen and I only lived about a block from each other. I often had coffee there in the morning with the other gals. One day, the gals started talking about men's pants. They didn't think the pants that American men wore looked that great. They much preferred the British ones that buttoned on the side. Well, I didn't, so we got into a friendly argument about, of all things, men's pants. Then somebody said something about Americans not being so friendly, and someone else turned to me and said, "Oh, but you let us get to know you. You're friendlier than most Americans."

I sat there in a state of shock, then let out a whoop. "Hey, you gals. I never worked so hard to get to know anybody as I did to get to know you girls." By then, we were all friends and could share a laugh. It felt great to have friends.

CRYSTAL CATHEDRAL, GARDEN GROVE, CALIFORNIA

I understood that. It does feel good to have friends. When I first arrived at DreamWorks, it was an effort to break in. Traveling as much as I did was a bit of a barrier. I had to be patient. Over time, I made my way.

Mom taught us the "secret" to friendship. She always said, "To have a friend, you've got to be a friend." That meant being loyal and trustworthy. Never revealing a confidence or talking behind your friend's back. The women she wrote to in the States were her friends until one or the other of them died; so were these "gals" Mom met in Kirkuk. Some of these kinships she "bequeathed" to me. Ava and Peggy outlived Mom, and I was fortunate to remain close to them until they passed.

Indeed, when Ava and Bobby adopted two children, they named their son after my dad and their daughter after my mom. My parents were so proud. I find it interesting that Ava's daughter, Lorraine, has much the same adventurous spirit as my mom. They were simpatico and got along very well. Now that these four great friends have all died, I think they would be happy that Ava's daughter, Lorraine, and I are continuing the grand tradition.

As an adult, I really came to know and love Peggy. She visited Mom in California, and Mom then went to Brisbane to visit her. Peggy returned to the States, where I picked up the torch and traveled to Peggy after she moved back to her hometown of Lismore, Australia. Indeed, I flew to see Peggy ten times in the ensuing years. Some of my favorite memories are walking the hills of Lismore at sunrise and enjoying Peggy's terrific cooking. We would talk for hours, take naps, and play Rummikub and Scrabble late into the night. It was a humbling experience when an eighty-, then ninety-something woman consistently beat me at the crossword board game. I was a bit luckier with the tile-pairing game of Rummikub. Peggy always said she didn't want to live to be a hundred, and she died at ninety-nine and six months, shortly after my last visit.

My sisters and I had played with Peggy's two sons in Iraq. Through my friendship with Peggy, I chanced to reconnect with her son Jon. Now Jon and I are also continuing the friendship established by our mothers.

One can guess by these long-term bonds what a terrific friend my mom must have been. These ladies lamented Mom's passing, and with their passing, my connection to Mom through them died as well. I valued those connections and felt the tremendous loss. I am not only grateful for Mom's teachings about friendship, but also for her example of what it means to be a true and loyal friend. Mom believed true friends maintained one's sanity — they cried with you, laughed with you — you supported one another through thick and thin.

I traveled so much at DreamWorks that I rarely saw my friends or went to church during those years, yet both remained constant. My church was the same one Mom and I attended, the Crystal Cathedral, in Garden Grove, California. Given that Peggy and Ava had been there with Mom and me on various trips to Southern California, it didn't surprise me that they all came to mind this one Sunday when I was in town actually attending a service. Thoughts of my friends loomed large that day too. I was quite simply amazed that all mine hadn't abandoned me from neglect. There were no candles at my church, but there was always a positive message, amazing music, and a stunning setting in which to reflect, heal, and grow. This day, I reflected. I was grateful that Mom not only taught me about being a good friend, but also that she lived long enough for me to grow from the childhood experience of her as "Mom" to the friendship we shared as adults.

Raggedy Ann and Andy/Lorraine and Don
Costume party for the adults

Unknown couple and Lorraine and Don
Formal dinner dance

Two unknown women, Ava Jamieson, and Lorraine
Another dinner party

6 "I could retire to my rocking chair, content"

LORRAINE — KIRKUK, 1956/1957

Living in town was very difficult because we were so far from the school, the club, the pool, everything. Don kept pushing to get us into camp. Finally, a day arrived after we had been there about three months when Don heard about a house becoming available, and he went, insisting we have it. I immediately started packing. Boy, I was going to get into that camp. It would be so good for the girls to be around other children and for us to be close to everything.

I called the day before to confirm the arrangements. "We are moving into number 7 Poplar Lane tomorrow — "

"Oh, no, you can't have that house," interrupted the man at the other end of the line. "That house has been assigned to someone else."

"Hey, wait a minute. I *am* coming into camp. I have four children, and I AM coming into camp!"

"Yes, but you can't have that one."

"All right, then, what house can I have?"

"Well, you are going to have to take number 4 Ridge Road."

I almost leaped through the phone to kiss that man because number 4 Ridge Road was the house where we spent Christmas day when we first arrived, and I had fallen in love with it. The Myerses were leaving Iraq, so it had just become available. The house stood by itself at the bottom of a long driveway. It had a large garden in the back surrounded by a high hedge with a small garden in front and a good-sized yard on the side, where we grew some vegetables. Eventually, we placed an unauthorized chicken coop in the side garden after I grew tired of cracking all the rotten eggs. If you walked through the side yard there was a wadi (small stream) that flowed by. The closest house was at the top of the drive, so it was lovely and private.

The house was all on one level, not nearly as big as our house in Kirkuk town, but I liked it so much better. As you entered the small foyer, directly in front of you were double doors that opened into the living room, which flowed through an archway into a formal dining room. To the left was a long hall with a very long closet for the children's toys and books and our linens and things. Further on, there were three bedrooms and two bathrooms.

To the right of the foyer was the very British double kitchen with giant pantry. If you proceeded out the side door of the kitchen, there was an enclosed courtyard, where the houseboy's bedroom and bathroom with a "hole-in-ground" toilet were located. In the foyer was a table with two phones: one was the oil line phone used to communicate between the various drilling and refining operations; the other was the company/general purpose phone that allowed you to call other houses in camp and for services like taxis and repairs.

The living room had a large, multipaned bow window, where I placed a small writing table. I could look out onto the veranda and beyond into the garden as I wrote my letters. One spring day, I sat watching a mongoose and her pups rolling and playing on the grass. I told Don about it, and he said it was a good thing because it meant we wouldn't have any snakes around. This room was the hub of our family's social life — I read to the girls in the comfy chair in the corner, schoolwork was completed at the large dining room table, meals consumed, visits by friends, parties, and everyday life occurred in those connected rooms.

Everything was so close. The girls would just walk up to the top of the drive, and a bus would pick them up for the five-minute ride to school. We could walk to the club, the pools, and the cinema. Like the house was the hub for our family's social life, the club was the hub for the camp's social life.

The club was an expansive multilevel building with a spacious round ballroom at its heart. It included a movie theater, a dining room, and a playhouse. The British were great at amateur theatrics, mounting a play a couple of times a year. There was a sweeping terrace off the ballroom that overlooked the massive pool with its high-diving platform (around five meters/fifteen feet). At the far end, a small covered wading pool for the little ones and an intermediate pool that ran across the narrow end of the massive pool. In addition, there was a small but excellent library with some limitations. It was run by a librarian who worked in an honorary capacity. Peggy Nees tells the story of a day when she asked for a certain book.

> I remember going in there one day to see if the library had a book I was interested in reading. The librarian was aghast that I would even ask for such a book. "Do you want to see me thrown out of the country?!"
> I couldn't fathom it. "What do you mean?"
> "The author of that book is a Jew. They wouldn't have let that book into the country."

This was a bit perplexing to us because Iraq was much more tolerant than other Arab countries. There were Jewish synagogues, Christian and Catholic churches along with the mosques, and a mixed population that worked and lived side by side.

The camp was divided into two sections, Baba East and Baba West, with the club at the center between the two. We lived in Baba West. Baba East had around sixty-three single-family homes, and Baba West had around eighty-two single-family homes. In addition, accommodations were available for bachelors and married bachelors, those men without their wives. There was the occasional house built in a style the British referred to as a "chumly," a house designed for three chums each with a bedroom and bath. Don stayed at one of those prior to our arrival in the Middle East, unless he was assigned to an oil rig too far from camp.

The camp was enclosed by a big fence all the way around, so you had no fear letting your children out to play because they weren't going to wander off. (Although later Pam told me she and her friend Carolyn found a way out into the desert by climbing through the large cement pipes that allowed the stream to flow through camp.) My one rule, the girls were to be sure and come home when the street lights came on.

The company provided all that we needed: laundry service for linens and the men's oil-soaked work clothes, gardeners, repair services, medical, transportation, and security. There was a wine and liquor steward who took regular trips to England, Rome, and France. He would bring back French wines and good liquor such as Pinch, a blended Scotch whiskey. We had five-star brandy that I had never seen in the States. We became so spoiled.

An expensive store called Spinneys was also provided by the company. I bought as little there as possible because I had seven mouths to feed and could do it cheaper by buying most of our food in town and at the souk. If I wanted to go anyplace in camp, to have a coffee with a friend, I would just pick up the phone and ask to have a taxi — no charge. The service ran from 7:30 a.m. to midnight, except when bringing the men home from their day's labors. If I wanted to go into Kirkuk or to the souk, all I had to do was to schedule a car and driver for the day. It was sure convenient.

It seemed most of the families were British, with some Americans, Scottish, French, and Dutch, all reflective of the multinational ownership of IPC. Lots of socializing went on. It took a while as an American to be accepted by the British, but once you broke through their reserve, you found some awfully nice people. It seemed, if you went to the house of a Brit, you would laugh and have fun. Yet when you went to the house of an American, all you did was talk about oil wells. As we were the only Americans with young children, we spent much of our time with British parents, and our circle of friends grew outward from there.

Again, I wrote to Margie about the social life.

> There is plenty to do here, but you can get tired of the club (the only place to eat out) and the cinema & the same people all the time. Also, the same 'company' talk. It's rather like being in the service with its command performances. A week ago, there was a cocktail party for Sir Cunningham, visiting from London; the next night a farewell cocktail party for our French General Manager; then there was a tea for the wife of a visiting Director from London, and a farewell coffee party for Madame Teyssot. Now I imagine when our new General Manager arrives we will start all over again with a cocktail party to meet them and a tea to get chummy with his wife. You know what I mean?
>
> Three weeks ago, we had 2 formal dinner parties, 1 dinner party, 1 cocktail party . . . all in one week. As soon as the baby lamb season comes, I'm reciprocating with an outside, cotton dress, Iraqi food party. Haha. But, we'd get mighty lonely if we didn't have the club and things going on.

Weekends were not Saturday and Sunday but Thursday and Friday as in the Muslim faith, so the men didn't work Thursday and Friday. Those were the nights people gave dinner parties or there were events that took place at the club. There were dances every Thursday night. Don was a terrific dancer, loved to dance (Deedee gets her love of dancing from him) and had real sex appeal. There was one Irish gal, Ann, who would ask Don to dance every time, and he never refused. One night, when she asked Don to dance, a German bachelor came and asked me to dance. No sooner did we step onto the dance floor than Herman began swinging me around going, "Ooh la la" one way, then he'd go, "Ooh la la" the other way.

Finally, I looked at him and I asked, "Herman, what are you doing?"

He swung me around again with another "Ooh la la."

"Ooh la la, what?" I stopped and turned around, and there was Ann melted into my husband.

"You can't put a piece of tissue paper between them. Look at her."

"Herman, don't worry about it, let's dance and enjoy ourselves."

"Are you not jealous?"

"No, Herman, I'm the one that takes him home to bed." He couldn't believe I could be so calm. He thought I should have gone and scratched her eyes out. But I couldn't think what good that would have done for either one of us.

After the dances ended, the tradition was to be invited to somebody's house or to invite some of the couples to your house. Each person had a specialty. When we went to the Carnegies', Eileen would have made Scotch eggs. If they came to the Newton house, they would get a classic American breakfast — scrambled eggs, bacon, toast, and coffee.

The men played golf on Friday, joining their wives and children at the club Friday noon for curry dinner. A long row of white-linen-covered tables was laden with crumbled egg, coconut, fried onions, cucumber, chopped tomatoes, three or four kinds of chutney, sultanas (light golden raisins), currants (dark raisins), peanuts, sliced banana, slivered almonds. There must have been twenty toppings or more. We would start with a small amount of rice topped with some very hot (spicy) Indian chicken curry. By the time we finished piling on the toppings, you couldn't see any signs of the curry below, or even the plate for that matter. It was hard to not lose a few bits on the way back to the table.

There were activities all week long. On Sunday night, I played whist at the club. It's like bridge only you change partners, and I could win at it. I never won at bridge and found that everyone was so super-duper serious about it. Tuesday night was Scottish dancing. Wednesday was tombola (a form of raffle game). I used to play it but got sick of the game.

There were movies every Monday, Thursday, and Friday night at the cinema. Some nights, after the evening cinema, Don and I would stop by the club for a drink and then walk home.

The children had their own activities. There was a movie every Friday afternoon. The children went to Sunday school on Thursday afternoon. Wednesday afternoon the older girls were in Brownies. Saturday afternoon was Pammy's dancing class.

I formed a co-op nursery group in Lakewood when Pammy was about eighteen months old and decided to begin one at the club. I started it for Pammy because she was driving me crazy, as usual. We had twelve children and twelve mothers and could have had a lot more, but our meeting space was too small. It was in the bar of the cinema. The company was great about providing supplies, but organizing it was a heck of a lot of work for me. We met Saturday through Wednesday from 8:30 to 11:00 a.m. It went over very well.

It was over 100 degrees in the summers, so the pool was our hub in the afternoons. The big meal was the noonday meal, and the men came home for it. Afterwards, the girls would nap, and I would make sandwiches to take with us to the pool. We would spend all afternoon there.

I'll never forget this one afternoon Ava showed up in a new white bikini she had just purchased in Baghdad. Ava had quite the figure and bore a strong resemblance to the glamorous movie star Ava Gardner. She was lovely. As I was drying off, I looked over and Ava was climbing the stairs out of the pool. I suddenly realized that white bathing suit had gone absolutely transparent. I grabbed a towel and went running for her, threw the towel around her, and said, "Come on in the dressing room, Ava."

"What for?"

"Just come with me."

I steered her in to the dressing room and stood her in front of the mirror, took the towel off, and she just gasped, "Ohhhhhhhhhh."

"Well, do what you have to do. I've got to go back to watch the children. Can't have them drown."

After that, the only time Ava ever wore that suit was when she and Bobby, Don, and I sneaked up to the pool and climbed the fence for a midnight swim. We weren't supposed to be there. We had no business being there of course, as we were feeling no pain. I'm surprised we didn't drown.

As you can see, there was lots of fun to be had if only you were willing to give it a go. Each time I got lonely for America, I would think about all the work at home. In Kirkuk, there were no dishes, no ironing, no peeling potatoes or veggies, no cleaning. Back home, there would be no houseboy to yell to, "Please bring me a cup of coffee" and have it served on a silver tray! Such luxury! I lived it up — I knew it wouldn't last forever. After this experience, I felt I could retire to my rocking chair, content.

ÉGLISE SAINT-PIERRE DE MONTMARTRE, PARIS, FRANCE

Life at DreamWorks had some of that "life in camp" feel about it. The studio sponsored parties by the lagoon for such occasions as

Cinco de Mayo and provided taxi vouchers if you had a bit too much to drink. The campus was secure with guards, and all our on-campus needs were met. There were gardeners and cleaners and trash collectors. There was even a doctor who came to the studio several days a week. Movies were screened in the company's theater, where family days happened on a regular basis complete with costumed characters.

DreamWorks had some lovely perks. It provided breakfast and lunch to all employees. There was a game room full of board games and interactive games, which only the animators seemed to use, with foosball tables outside. I was always too busy for such fun, but if I had it to do over, I would have made some time. Every care had been taken from the interior lighting to the design of the campus to make it a happy place of creativity.

Our CEO, Jeffrey Katzenberg, invited his fellow industry titans to come and talk with us. One time, Jeffrey interviewed George Miller, the Australian film producer-director of such animated and live-action movies as *Happy Feet*, the *Mad Max* series, and *Babe*. Another time he interviewed George Lucas of *Star Wars* fame. Jeffrey held town hall meetings where he discussed the successes and concerns of the company and where we could ask questions. We got a glimpse into his day and travels through his email blogs. His time was so valuable that when he visited our distribution partners across the globe, his schedule was timed to the five minutes. He was tireless in his efforts for DreamWorks, and many of us worked tirelessly in return.

There is something magical about being a part of Hollywood and the entertainment business. Life at a studio is a pretty cool thing. Studios are designed to be safe places for celebrities and creative people alike. Both Paramount and DreamWorks have beautiful, if different, campuses. Paramount's is famous, awash in Hollywood history. It has always been about live-action productions, which means it has over thirty sound stages, woodworking shops, even a small fire department, a New York street outdoor set, and the iconic blue sky and the wrought iron gates that Norma Desmond drove through in *Sunset Boulevard*. You needed a golf cart to traverse its fifty-six-acre lot. When guests came to my office at Paramount, they could see the Hollywood sign through the windows behind my desk. It never failed to impress my guests or, for that matter, me. I felt very privileged every day when I drove on the lot and always felt a sense of wonder.

DreamWorks Animation had a beautiful Tuscan-style campus in Glendale on thirteen acres. Animation studios don't need large sound stages for filming as their creative process involves computers, sound recording studios, and motion capture studios. It was full of olive trees and centered around a lovely large koi pond fed by a stream that originates at the back of campus. As you followed the flowing water, the grounds became more rustic and the traveler ended up at the source, an area I used to think of as "Yosemite" — a place of large granite boulders amid long grasses. One can easily walk the campus in under ten minutes. When I finished a report or a presentation, I often took a walk to clear my head and get ready for the next one lined up on my desk.

One can imagine my disappointment when several of the studio's departments, including mine, had to move off campus, about five miles away, for two years while the studio built a new building to house its growing staff. One could easily feel disconnected with the place where it all happens. There were lots of times when I skipped fun events because it wasn't worth the drive, where before I could pop down from my office and spend a few minutes. So I fully understood how my mom felt living so far away from the main camp and the effort and time it took to participate in activities there.

I could also imagine my mom's excitement at moving into camp from her isolation in Kirkuk town when I found myself packing up my office before leaving for my next junket. The new construction at the studio was complete. We were being repatriated to the DreamWorks campus during my trip. The boxes would be stacked in my new office awaiting my return. I was thrilled to be going back.

This trip was longer than usual, two weeks. I was going to Madrid, Paris, and then on to London. I found myself with a weekend in Paris. I decided to see Sacré-Cœur Basilica. On the way there, I chose a route that allowed me to climb the famous steps I had seen in so many paintings and postcards, the steep steps of Montmartre.

They had that classic 1940s film noir feel about them with their deep shadows. I wasn't disappointed as the old lampposts and lacy trees gave me the feeling of being transported in time into a movie scene from a bygone era.

It was lovely to be a part of a great studio like DreamWorks and have the opportunity to climb this grand stairway in Paris. When I reached the top, I was not directly in front of Sacré-Cœur but close enough to see the crowds of tourists milling about. I was not in the mood for crowds. Instead I walked through a charming outdoor area full of artist and vendor stalls where I bought a 6" × 6" abstract oil painting of the Eiffel Tower and headed toward this older church located to the side of Sacré-Cœur.

The church was called Église Saint-Pierre de Montmartre. It dated from the twelfth century and was much older than Sacré-Cœur. My eyes immediately went to the front of the church with its decorative altar and the stained-glass windows in the apse behind. I had done a ton of walking that day, so I sat and rested. My mind drifted back in time.

This was an odd moment of gratitude for me because usually I delighted in thinking about my mom and the gifts she gave me. But today, I kept drifting to how grateful I felt working in the entertainment industry and especially for my job at DreamWorks. Finally, I said to her spirit, "Well, Mom, we both have been on grand adventures, and I believe I will feel the way you did when you said in your letter, 'After this experience I [too] could retire to my rocking chair, content.'"

Chuckling, I thought. "Well, maybe not." I could never imagine myself in a rocking chair. Life was much too joyful. Ah, but the "content" part, now *that* I could appreciate very much. "Appreciate" . . . that was it! My mom appreciated everything and passed that appreciation on to us. When I stopped to light my candle on this extraordinary day, I thanked her for teaching me to appreciate and *feel* appreciative, for indeed I did.

Hassan and his bicycle

7 "So Hassan came to us"

There was a couple in camp, Maria and Max MacCune, who were childless. Maria became one of my best friends after we arrived. She was a Spanish dancer who married an American driller. Her accent was so thick I couldn't understand everything she said. She had only started to learn English four years before I met her. Maria was something, though. She was the quintessential Latin spitfire!

Maria took quite a liking to Pam. Within the first two months of us being in Iraq, she had already talked me into letting Pam stay with her and Max for a couple of weeks. That was how their houseboy, Hassan, got to know us. Just after we moved into camp, the MacCunes went on a four-month leave. Hassan's reputation as a hard worker meant lots of people wanted him during the MacCunes' leave. Maria decided to ask Hassan who he would like to work for.

"Does Pammy's mother have a good boy?" Hassan asked.

"She certainly does not."

"I want to go work for Pammy's mother."

"But, Hassan, that's six people!" Maria exclaimed.

"I don't care. I want to go work there."

Because of Hassan's request, Max and Maria came and asked me and Don if we would have him. Oh boy, would I? I would have jumped through hoops to have this boy. He was that good. Yes, yes, yes!

While the MacCunes were on leave, they got word that they were being transferred to Basrah. Basrah is a city at the southernmost tip of Iraq by the Persian Gulf and is about four hundred miles from Kirkuk. Hassan refused to go. Hassan was a Persian from Iran and in Iraq illegally. He had a brother nearby in Kirkuk but no one in Basrah. Yet there were rules about loaned houseboys. You were never to entice them to stay in any way. You were never to give them any gifts. They were to go back to the family who loaned them to you.

Maria was certain we had done something underhanded and was spitting mad. We assured her that we had paid him exactly what they had specified, never given him a gift or any inducement to stay, but still he refused to leave. Max came over to talk with him. Hassan told Max there was no way he would go to Basrah. Afterwards, Max said, "Okay, he's yours." Max and a still-furious Maria went off to Basrah. So Hassan came to us.

After Max and Maria left, we bought Hassan a bicycle so he could go into Kirkuk town to visit his brother, and we gave him a raise. We felt he deserved it after working for us for nine dinars a month (about twenty-five U.S. dollars). The McCunes had been paying Hassan seven or eight dinars a month but asked us to pay more because of the extra people. As the years went by, we gave him more raises; he deserved them.

Hassan had been with us a while when I went in the kitchen one day and saw him eating from a tin plate, drinking his chai from a tin cup, and eating with a tin fork. I asked, "Hassan, what are you eating on that for?"

"Boys eat off this," he replied. "Always English house make boys eat off this." Also, lots of people brought special, cheaper food and rice and had their boys cook their food separate.

I reached up in the cupboard. "Hassan, you help me prepare the food. You help me cook the food. And you will eat the same food at this house. Never again let me see you eat off of that tin plate." I emptied his food onto a regular china plate like we used. I poured his chai into a china cup and took his fork away. "You use the forks in our silverware drawer and never again do you eat with that."

The boys had a couple of hours off in the afternoons. They would sometimes visit each other. I continued, "I'll tell you another thing. When you have guests and want to make them chai, you make them chai. You take the cups from the cupboard here, you take this tray here, and you take it to your room. If it's summer, make them a cold drink with ice in it. There is lemonade, soda, Squash — whatever you want, make it for them. If there's cookies here, take a plate out there too." Well, by the time I was done, he was speechless. I think Hassan became my friend that day.

I taught Hassan how to make breakfast for Don and the girls and get them off to work and school before I emerged from the bedroom. I believe my family was grateful for that because I was downright disagreeable first thing in the morning. When I arose and came into the living room, Hassan would silently bring in a little silver tray with a jar of instant coffee, a little silver pot with hot water, a china cup and saucer, and a glass of ice water. By this time, he had cleaned the front of the house already, so he could close the doors and go and clean the bedrooms in the back of the house.

Hassan had gotten wise to me pretty quickly and knew that I was not in a very good humor before my coffee. Every day, the company sent a sweeper and gardener to the house. Occasionally, Hassan would meet me in the living room without my coffee with a complaint.

"Memsaab, sweeper out there very lazy. Laying down. Gardener don't do this or that." I would shoot out the veranda door and tell the sweeper what to do and get the gardener going. I'd come in spitting mad, and Hassan would be standing there, smiling, with my coffee on the little silver tray.

One day, I told him, "Hassan, please wait until I have my coffee, and then tell me problems."

"Oh, no, Memsaab, I not do that. Before Memsaab have

coffee, plenty mean. Go take care of things. After Mem-saab have coffee, ha! Good. Plenty good. I not bring coffee to you before. When I have trouble, you take care of it. Then coffee."

Occasionally, one of the women would ring for morning coffee. I was not much of a morning person, as you now know, so if it was too early, Hassan would cover for me. I didn't real-ize anyone was wise to my clever ruse until years later when Peggy told me how she uncovered my little deception.

> *On occasion, I would think, "Oh, I'll have Lor-raine out for morning tea." I'd ring Lorraine's house, where Hassan would answer and tell me, "Oh, Mem-saab in shower." I'd ring back ten minutes later, and Memsaab still in the shower. So that went on several times, and then the coin dropped. Memsaab wasn't in the shower. Memsaab was in bed — and it was ten in the morning! Eventually, Memsaab surfaced and we'd have our tea, although it was probably afternoon tea by this time. I would have been in bed too then if I'd had a Hassan. But I didn't have a Has-san. I had a George. I had to get up and get my boys off to school myself.*

Then there was the time we had a dinner party at the house. I made lemon meringue pies for dessert. When I looked in the refrigerator in the morning, there were still one and one-half pies left, but they were cut in squares! I looked at them and then I looked at Hassan and said, "Has-san, why in the world would you cut a lemon pie like this? You know how to cut a pie, and yet you cut it into squares?"

"Memsaab, I no cut those pies. You did."

I thought, "Uh-oh." Apparently, it was quite the evening, and perhaps I'd had a bit too much to drink. Boy, did I slink out of that kitchen!

Before we went on our first leave, I had Hassan stand on a piece of paper and drew his foot because he had a wide foot. The one thing he really wanted was a pair of shoes. So I bought him a pair of Florsheim shoes. I mean good ones. He was so pleased when we got back with the shoes. He wore them into town to show them to his brother. He came back with an old pair on. I said, "What happened to your new shoes?"

"My brother liked them. I had to give them to him."

I asked, "Why?" Apparently, anytime you told an Arab you liked something, they'd take the shirt off their back and hand it to you. Well, I told him, I said, "You go back and tell your brother that you've broken the Memsaab's heart, that she carried those shoes all the way from California for you." So the next week when he went into Kirkuk town, he came back with his new shoes.

Over the course of the next few years, we brought him other gifts. Things like a jacket, scarf and gloves, a hat, because it would be cold some nights when he came back on his bicycle. Every time I gave him anything, I'd say, "You break the Memsaab's heart if you give this away." And he held on to them.

Iraqis made tea in an implement called a samovar. It had a space where you put the water that surrounded a pipe that held hot coals. Then you would put a chimney on it. The charcoal would heat the water. When the water was hot, you opened the spigot to allow the hot water to fill the tea pot. While the tea was simmering, the pot was placed on top of the pipe that held the charcoals. Of course, Hassan said the tea was far better from a samovar.

Well, I didn't have one. I learned he spent eighteen months trying to talk a family in a mud hut out of their samovar. He wanted to buy it as a gift for me. One evening he came home from Kirkuk town cold and miserable on his bicycle. On the front he had a samovar. Hassan paid one dinar and eight hundred fils (a dinar was $2.80, so he paid about $4.60) for this heirloom. I was delighted with it. When I came home to the States, I couldn't see myself going out on the patio and putting in charcoal to make my tea this way, so I had it converted into a lamp for my living room.

Hassan didn't get sick very often, but when he got a headache or a stomachache, you would have thought he was dying. I'd come out in the kitchen, and his face would be long. "Oh, Memsaab, no feel well."

"Don't worry, Hassan, I'll fix it." I would go in and get an aspirin, and I would give him one. Then I had some vitamin pills that were different colors. I would take a couple of them in the kitchen and cut them in two, add in another aspirin cut in half, lay them in a little saucer. Then I'd tell him, "Now, you take this in two hours, and two hours later, you take that."

Well, he'd be racing around there, headache gone after the first aspirin. Once he took his medicine, he'd come to me and say, "Memsaab, you better than any doctor. I tell you, when you go back to America, you go to school maybe one month, two month, be doctor. Good one."

Hassan was the good one, and he was good with the children. He could iron. I tried to stop him from ironing the girls' underwear and socks, but he would even iron their little socks. He washed the floors on his hands and knees, no matter how hard I tried to get him to use a mop. He insisted. He saw to every need. All our doorknobs, window knobs were solid brass that had to be polished. About the time I'd look at the brass and think, "Oh, I'd better tell him next week to polish them," by God, the next day, they were all polished, and I never had to say a word. Those things shone. Our whole house shone. I was so pleased. I would say I'm not the best housekeeper, but I'd tell you that we had the best-kept house in Kirkuk. We loved Hassan, not just because he was a terrific houseboy, but because he was our friend and a part of the family. And he returned every kindness we bestowed in spades.

ÉGLISE SAINT-ROCH, PARIS, FRANCE

Unfortunately, I keep a messy office. Before I would leave on my overseas trips, necessity required me to clean up my cluttered desk. Even with the expansion DreamWorks had recently undergone, there was no extra space. If you were traveling, your office became the temporary office to a visiting member of the team visiting from another country.

It turned out there was something of the same thing at IPC. It was customary to save one's leave or vacation for a couple of years. This would give you time for a long holiday, three or four months or more, to see the world and return to one's home country. You packed all your personal things in one room of your home and locked the door. That would allow a visiting wife and children to enjoy living together as a family in your house. It was also customary if you went on leave to give your houseboy to someone as the MacCunes did with Hassan to us. This was so the houseboy would have work and continue to get paid.

I don't know what happened to Hassan's predecessor, Asa. Mom never said. But like Peggy, I did not have a Hassan, or any help for that matter, at DreamWorks. But oh, how I wished I did. The assistant (not that I am equating an assistant with a houseboy, just with the idea of some help) I had been promised when I started never materialized. It would have made a huge difference in my life. My assistants at Paramount handled a phenomenal amount of work. We were a team.

Another challenge I faced was that I never learned to type. I am of an age that when I went into the working world, a secretary would have been a likely role for me, even with my college degree. I figured, if I couldn't type, then I could never be made a secretary. I never did become a secretary, but it has been a self-made handicap to not type well in today's business world. More than correspondence (most of which I did via email anyway) at DreamWorks, it was the travel, the expense reports, all the presentations, and report after report after report that made me regret my decision not to learn to type. Some days it felt like we did so many reports, it was a wonder we could get any other work done.

Several years into the job, I challenged my boss's boss, the group president, when she asked how it was going, "It makes no sense for you to pay me what you do to do expense reports, book travel, make appointments. I could accomplish so much more if I had a little support. Furthermore, I believe the company has not followed through on its promise of an assistant because you know I will do whatever it takes to get the job done, no matter how many hours, and that is simply not fair." Well, my little speech accomplished nothing, so I soldiered on, leaving for Paris the next day.

My friend Patrick in Paris was the controller of a chain of boutique hotels with one, Hotel Brighton, located on the rue de Rivoli. It was opposite the Tuileries Gardens, which stretched in front of the Louvre, and was within walking distance of our new French agent's office. The hotel was in such an amazing location. I was delighted when Patrick was able to arrange lodging within my expense budget so I could stay close by. After a busy day of meetings, I was walking away from our agent's offices down the rue du Faubourg Saint-Honoré, which became rue Saint-Honoré. Not realizing I had overshot my hotel, I ended up in front of a Catholic church, Église Saint-Roch. Of course, I wandered in.

The church was full of wonderful carvings, like stone scenes of the stations of the cross, so many statues, painted ceilings, stained glass windows. Everywhere I looked there was some wonder. As I walked forward, I was enchanted by an immense sculpture of golden crepuscular rays emanating from a round stained-glass window. Carved white clouds chock full of winged cherubs were spread among the beams. Goodness, what a find this church was! I laughed when I learned the Marquis de Sade was married in this church in 1763. It seemed somehow appropriate for the situation I was in at the studio. I felt a bit like I was being tortured by having no help. But my favorite of all was a small statue of Saint Expedite, patron saint of expeditious solutions, against procrastination, among other things. I sat on one of the rather uncomfortable wooden chairs with their woven seats to ponder this. I was a procrastinator of the highest order. This book I wanted to write about my mother was still undone. I needed an expeditious solution for all the work I had to do and all the ideas I'd yet to pursue.

Mom wasn't a procrastinator like me, and she had Hassan. Hassan was her cohort in getting everything done around the house, while helping to maintain her reputation. I really loved working in a team. Now my role was very solitary. As I sat there, I realized the desire for an assistant had more to do with having a partner than simply getting more things accomplished at work. I loved that Mom and Hassan had so much fun together. Later I applied this concept of a team to make this book happen. We used to say at Dream-Works, "It takes teamwork to make the dream work."

On this day as I lit my candle, I was grateful that Hassan had come to us, that he was so conscientious and diligent in his work, and that Mom was the kind of "boss" that engendered such loyalty. Their easy relationship gave us all such a brilliant experience and made our house a happy house. Thank you, Mom, for creating such a pleasant home.

Pammy

8 "She was a little demon!"

Perhaps a little prelude to this chapter is in order. I already had a reputation for being a bit of a troublemaker before we ever arrived in Iraq. Mom even called me the female version of Dennis the Menace to a newspaper reporter after I jumped thirty feet off a cliff into an ocean shipping channel in Long Beach when I was just eighteen months old. The newspaper headline read, "Heroic Father Saves Baby."

I was walking at nine months, talking at eleven months, and toilet-trained by the time I was a year old. It wasn't that I was so brilliant. I had three older sisters, who interacted with me all the time, and a mother who was tired of washing diapers. I refused to take a nap and would go until I dropped — headfirst into the mashed potatoes and gravy. I "feeded" the goldfish cigarette ashes from the ashtray, resulting in their tragic demise. When I was still in diapers, my parents woke up wondering if an intruder was in the house. It was just me with my own version of a Slip 'N Slide made from butter, cream, and eggs spread all over the kitchen floor. Then there was the time I escaped with my little red wagon from a locked, gated garden surrounded by a six-foot fence and crossed two busy streets to be with my sisters at school. I could go on, but I think you get the idea.

And my reputation seemed to be confirmed by all of Mom's friends. You know you must have been something as a child when people look at you all grown up and say. "Oh, you turned out *so* nice." As if it was the most surprising thing ever that I didn't turn out to be, oh, I don't know, a mass murderer or something. Jeez.

LORRAINE — KIRKUK, 1957

The only problem Hassan and I had was when I would

spank Pammy. She needed spanking, believe me. She was a little demon! The routine was that I would spank her when she did something wrong and put her in her room. One day, after I put Pam in her room, I heard whispering in the kitchen. I went in. There was Hassan with Pammy sitting in his lap, having made her a little demitasse cup of chai, drying the tears on her face, and softly saying, "Pammy, you be good girl. Don't upset Mama. You be good girl."

"Hassan! What is *she* doing in here?"

"Pammy be good girl now, Memsaab. Pammy be good girl."

Pammy readily agreed with Hassan, "Yes, Pammy be good girl."

"Hassan, when I spank her and put her in her room, I will go get her." I took her back to her room. From that day on, anytime I spanked Pam, he wouldn't go get her. Instead, when I spanked her, Hassan would go into the kitchen and start slamming the cupboards. Whatever cupboard he went into, he slammed that door.

One day, I got tired of that. Pammy was in her bedroom, and he was slamming cupboards. I went out there and opened every cupboard door and slammed each as hard as I could. Hassan was standing there, looking at me in a state of shock. I turned to him. "You want to see somebody slam a cupboard? I'll slam a cupboard. Now when I spank Pammy, you don't come out in this kitchen and slam these cupboards!" We didn't have any more slamming cupboards after that.

Pammy adored Hassan and he spoiled her, but there were times when she could be even too much for him. One Friday after her sisters were away at boarding school, Pam and I met Don at the golf club for a meal. Pam was about six years old at the time. Afterwards, I was going to get a cab and drop Pam off for the children's matinee at the cinema. An Englishman, whose wife was going to play a round of golf, was taking his son to the cinema so he suggested,

"I'm headed home. Why don't you stay with Don and I'll drop Pammy off with my son? After the show, you can pick her up or I will send her home in a taxi." I liked the idea of staying for drinks with Don and thankfully agreed.

A couple of hours later, we got this call at the club from Hassan. He called the Sahb and wanted him to come home right now! He was so upset: "Plenty trouble with Pammy!" Of course, we had to get right home.

There was another English friend who had joined us at the club and quickly offered to drive us rather than wait for a taxi. So off we went to the house. I made our guest a drink while Don went into the kitchen to talk with Hassan. Apparently, Pam had tried smoking at the little boy's house, and when she came home, she took one of our cigarettes, lit a match, and got to puffing. Naturally, we had cigarettes lying around. We never thought to put them up. We had never caught any of the girls smoking. Then she showed Hassan what she was doing, and he had a fit. Pammy wasn't about to put that cigarette out. So after threatening her, he called us to come home from the club.

Now Don mixed a drink. I went to get Pam, who had hightailed it down the hall to her bedroom when she heard us drive up. I brought her into the living room. Her dad talked with her, then I talked with her that she shouldn't smoke. Pam asked, "Why can't I?"

I explained, "I'll tell you, Pam, when you can afford to buy your own cigarettes, you can smoke all you want. But you have to buy your own." (This was before we knew cigarettes were bad for you.)

Pam considered this and then asked, "How much are cigarettes, Mum?" I told her they were fifty fils a pack (about fourteen cents). Pam excused herself, went down the hall, and brought back fifty fils from her piggy bank and handed it to me. "Here, Mum, next time you are in town, buy me up a pack." She took one look at my face and was off down the hall. Well, I'll tell you, I shot out of that chair and was right after her. And when I caught her, boy, did she get a spanking.

In the meantime, our British friend, whose name escapes me, is trying to keep from releasing peals of laughter during this exchange. And Don was trying to restrain himself as well. It seems my attempt at reasoning didn't turn out so well, and I had to resort to the usual punishment, a spanking, in the end.

She just did the most surprising things. One day, when I was bathing Pam, I was washing around her ear and she let out a yip. I looked in her ear and could see something lodged inside. The next morning, I took her to the doctor, and he pulled a wad of cotton out of her ear. How it got there, how long it had been there, I don't know.

A few months later, I was washing her face and she let out another yip. This time, it was her nose that was sensitive. I looked up her nose and something was there. Back to the doctor we go. Turns out she had a bean, a white bean, up her nose. It was starting to sprout! She never said a word. It must have hurt, but she probably knew I would think that was awfully stupid.

When Pam was in kindergarten, one day her teacher, June Ambrosek, called to tell us about her latest misdeed. As the children were coming in from recess, each one jumped as they came in the door. There were two doors to each classroom, so June just sneaked around to the other door to see what was going on. There was Pammy standing by the door, pinching all the little bottoms of her fellow classmates as they entered. Poor Pammy, she just got in trouble all the time.

ST. MARY'S CATHEDRAL, SYDNEY, AUSTRALIA

Time-outs and sitting in the corner were not the kind of discipline my parents employed. This was a different time. Our mouths were washed out with soap if we said a "bad" word, and we received spankings for all else. We were never hit with an object like a belt or a hairbrush, but then my dad was very strong as an oil driller, so his spankings were plenty. Indeed, Mom saved the biggest fear — "Just wait until your father gets home" — for when we had really messed up. We knew a Dad spanking was much worse than a Mom spanking.

This one time when I was about three or four, I had misbehaved and was facing just such a fate, so I devised a cunning plan. When I heard Dad come home, I quickly went to my room to put on every pair of underwear in my drawer. In between each pair of pants, I inserted a Little Golden Book. I probably had six to eight layers of book/underwear, book/underwear before being summoned. Mom said I came down the hall waddling like a duck because my many pairs of underpants hung almost down to my knees while my dress stuck out like a bustle in back. Dad picked me up and put me across his lap, and his hand landed with a thud. I didn't feel a thing and felt pretty clever until he said, "What have we got here?" That time I got a bare-bottom spanking. I didn't try that again.

Then there was an occasion where Mom, in her efforts to mold me into a reasonable adult, executed one of her more extreme disciplinary efforts. I was probably around four. Because my sisters were in school and I was not, I was fortunate to travel with Mom and Dad to Beirut on a short holiday. Every day at 5:00 p.m., Mom dressed me in one of my little party frocks with a big bow tied in back, and we all went downstairs for cocktails. Folks paid a lot of attention to me because I had blonde ringlets down my back and would dance and talk with just about anyone. When 5:00 p.m. rolled around the day after we returned to Kirkuk, I dutifully put on one of my party dresses, open in the back with the ties streaming behind me, appeared in the living room, and announced, "Time for cocktails!" Something about this effort did not sit well with my mom. She rose from her chair and dragged me screaming into the bathroom where she cut off all of my hair!

When I was in my forties, I finally asked her why she'd done that. "You were acting prissy. And I wasn't going to have a prissy conceited daughter."

"Surely there was another way?"

"Well, you aren't conceited, are you?" she huffed.

I thought for a moment. "No, I don't think I am."

"Then it worked." There was no arguing with her logic. That was the end of the conversation. I believe, in her mind, the ends justified the means. I had obviously triggered something deep inside her as this was not her norm.

I think I have always been a bit lawless or headstrong. Luckily, it rarely showed up on the job. I remember a trip to Australia when my boss with our agents arranged a surprise birthday luncheon for me. While she was extolling my virtues, I was appreciative but laughing inside, thinking how surprised my colleagues would be if they only knew what a devil child I had been.

After the day was done, I begged off dinner and went for a walk. Sydney is such an easy city to get around in, especially the central business district, where my hotel was located. I headed over to the botanical gardens and then up toward Hyde Park, near where St. Mary's Cathedral was located. Kirkuk was definitely on my mind. I was going to fly up to visit Mom's friend Peggy Nees in Lismore for the weekend, and I was having dinner in Sydney with her son Jon the night before. I was very attached to Peggy. She was a direct link to Mom, and I so enjoyed my time in her company.

St. Mary's, as the name suggests, is dedicated to Mary, mother of Jesus. It is the center of Australian Catholicism. It is a massive Gothic sandstone structure built of the rock on which Sydney rests. Here I was in a mom church. How perfect. Recalling my less-than-stellar childhood, I remembered Mom often said, "If I'd had you first, you wouldn't have any sisters." That statement gave me a lot to be grateful for as I lit a candle this day. First, that I was *not* born first. Second, that my job at DreamWorks had brought me to Australia, where I could see Peggy again. Third, that my mom was a rock of a mother, tough enough and stubborn enough to take on the challenge of raising me. Thanks, Mom, for wrangling me into a semidecent human being!

Lorraine
Always reading

9 "I think Memsaab go crazy in the head tonight!"

It was my first trip to Germany in over twenty years. I had last stepped onto German soil when I was a teenager with my parents visiting Kathy, who was studying at the University of Tübingen. This time, I had just a night and part of a day in Cologne to meet with Toys "R" Us to discuss a retail promotion around our fun new animated comedy *Madagascar*. My boss and I were staying in an absolutely beautiful hotel across the Rhine from the city center. When I looked out across the water, I saw the rising spires of a magnificent cathedral. I vowed to research a hotel closer that would allow me to visit it on my next trip.

When I got back to Los Angeles, I learned this cathedral was officially called Hohe Domkirche Sankt Petrus but was more commonly referred to as Cologne Cathedral. It is renowned for its Gothic architecture and is reported to be the most visited site in Germany. It has to have one of the longest build times ever, almost 632 years from start to completion. Two 515-foot spires dominate its landscape. Apparently, it is possible to climb them, but I never had the time. The medieval builders had planned a grand structure to house the remains of the three wise men, the Magi, and it certainly achieves its goal, having been selected as a World Heritage site. I couldn't wait to see it.

My next trip was in the fall. It was cold and gray in Cologne, but I didn't care. I couldn't believe my good fortune. I had secured a room in the first-class Dom Hotel on the plaza of the cathedral. One of the first things I would do on arriving in any room was to look out and see what view awaited me. I opened the drapes, and much to my delight this small room actually looked out onto the plaza. There in front of me were the towering spires and pointy pinnacles of the Gothic masterpiece. It couldn't have been more than a couple of hundred yards away.

I decided I would leave the drapes open all night so I could fall asleep and wake to this commanding view.

To relax before bedtime, I often read. I started reading a funny, funny book by Janet Evanovich that made me laugh out loud. I was sure glad I was up a couple of floors, so hopefully no one could see me prostrate in a shower of ongoing giggles. People would wonder about this insane woman if they could see me doubled over on my pillows hysterically laughing all by myself — especially in Germany, where everything was neat and clean and orderly. I don't mean that as a criticism in any way. I love Germany, and the German people have been very kind to me. I have many friends there. But it is more formal there. Suit and ties, addressing each other formally (Herr Doktor), where degrees are listed on one's business card. I didn't want to become the poster child for the crazy American who sometimes did not display a proper sense of decorum, respect, and appropriateness.

And then I remembered Mom's story of the time our houseboy, Hassan, thought she was crazy for precisely the same reason.

LORRAINE — KIRKUK, 1957

One night, Don was called out to the rig. I put the girls to bed and didn't have anything to do. Then I remembered I did have a new book from the club library. It was called *Forty Plus and Fancy Free* by Emily Kimbrough. Well, it turned out that darned book was one of the funniest books I had ever read. And I wish I had that book to this day. It was a story about two American women who went on a trip to Europe. When one of them was in a bath in Rome, she pulled a chain not knowing what it did. The next thing she heard was a man's voice standing next to her saying, "Yes, madame?" You know, like, "You rang." She was horrified because she didn't realize she had rung for the hall porter and well, of course, she was naked.

I laughed my way through that darned book, sitting there all by myself while Hassan was ironing in the kitchen. It's seldom that I get a book where I laugh out loud, but this one, I was laughing out loud. And the next thing I see is Hassan peeking around through the dining room. "Memsaab, you want chai?"

"No, no."

He went back to the kitchen, and I let out another laugh. Back he comes. "Memsaab, you all right?"

"Oh, yes, Hassan, I am just fine."

"You're sure you don't want chai?"

"No, no."

"You want something?"

"No, really nothing."

What I really wanted was to keep reading my book. So he goes back out again. The next time I laughed, he came in and stood at the dining room entrance to the living room. "Memsaab, nobody in this room. Just you. Why you go ha-ha, hee-hee?"

Knowing Hassan could not read or write, I explained, "Hassan, I'm reading a book. Very funny, it makes me laugh." He looked at me strangely and walked back to the kitchen, but every once in a while, I'd see him peeking at me. Finally, I gave up and went to bed. I told Hassan to go to bed. But unbeknownst to me, he waited up until Don got home around midnight.

"Sahb, I got something to tell you."

"What?" Don asked.

Hassan pointed to his head making a circle with his finger and announced, "I think maybe Memsaab go crazy in the head tonight."

"What happened, Hassan?"

"Memsaab no talk on the telephone. No person in that living room. Nobody her talk to. Her and book. Go 'ha-ha, hee-hee' all evening! I think maybe something wrong," he reported.

Don reassured him, "That's all right, Hassan. You go to bed. I'll take care of it."

The next morning as we were lying in bed, Don asked,

"Honey, what were you doing last night?"

Excitedly, I told him, "Oh, Don, I'm reading the funniest book. You've got to read it. It struck me as so funny that I laughed all evening." Then he told me what happened with Hassan when he came home. "What did you do?" I asked.

"I told him not to worry. Go to bed. What was new? Memsaab crazy anyway."

I picked up the pillow and threw it at him!

HOHE DOMKIRCHE SANKT PETRUS (COLOGNE CATHEDRAL), GERMANY

What Mom found hard to believe was that Hassan just couldn't understand that anything that could be read could be that funny. Reading was one of the most joyous things in our house. Books and comic books brought from the States were everywhere. We had no TV. Playing together, games, and books were our entertainment.

When Kathy was a toddler and still sleeping in a crib, Mom would announce bedtime, and Kathy would paddle to her room and throw all the books she could gather into the crib. Mom would push them aside and place her in the middle. Many a morning, Mom woke to find Kathy with a corner of a book imprinted on her cheek.

When we first moved to the Middle East and were living in Kirkuk town, I needed some playmates. My sisters were in school, but I was only three years old. Two young French children lived close by, and my mom was delighted. She thought I would learn some French, while they might learn some English. No such luck. Somehow, we jabbered away in our respective languages and understood each other "perfectly." The boy loved my Little Golden Book *The Little Engine That Could*. Every day when he came over, he would find it in the pile and make known to my mom that he wanted her to read it to us. She did, often twice a day for months. She figured that she must have had enough animation and realistic choo-choo sounds to make it fun for him.

Mom read to us every night before bed. I don't know how many times she read us *Heidi*. The rule was one chapter, and as it came to the end, we would hold our breaths, hoping she would go on. She admitted in later years that when it was a particularly exciting point in the book, she too wanted to find out what happened, so she would go on. When she finished, Mom would feign shock, exclaiming, "You were such good girls tonight I forgot to stop and read *two* chapters!" We thought we had pulled one over on her, and it made us want to be good for each story time.

Clever Mother.

My sisters and I share a love of books and reading. Books were and are my companions when traveling. I could get lost in some mystery or other, some romance or other, some historical novel or other. Mom's excitement was contagious. Often, she would stop when a new custom was revealed in the text and talk about how interesting it was the way they do "that" in whatever time, place, or culture. I have books everywhere and always one or two when I travel. My schedule was such that I didn't have much time to read, but even a chapter or two here and there was a treat.

So here I was in Germany, with a book that made me laugh out loud, and a view of a magnificent cathedral. I made my wake-up call for an hour earlier than necessary just so I could walk to the shopping street close by to have a coffee and pastry before spending twenty minutes or so inside. As I fell asleep staring at the cathedral, I knew just what I was going to thank my mother for when I lit a candle in the morning — my love of reading.

The day dawned. Fresh from my coffee, I stopped as I rounded the corner to look upon the sobering, magnificent giant in the chilly gray light of the early fall morning. The cathedral's long shadow stretched across the square and up the nearby buildings. The ornately carved façade was blackened, perhaps from the fires in the war but most certainly from age and pollution. On the right, there was construction on what looked like it might become a gift shop or welcome center. I ascended the cathedral steps much more subdued than the night before, that feeling of reverence descending over me as it often did when I went into a church. As I ventured inside, I began to take in some of the views. I wandered through the nave toward the transept. There were most assuredly too many sights for the time I had allowed (although on subsequent visits, I was able to discover more).

It was so easy to lose track of time, and I realized DWA's German agent, Joachim, would be arriving soon. Quickly, my mind turned back to Mom. I went to one of the places where I could light a candle. A smile crossed my face as I recalled the night before and all the hours spent lost in the other worlds that books provided. I thought too about authors everywhere who write words that teach us, enlighten us, entertain us, reveal hidden truths, and give perspective, hope, and encouragement. I had a mother who didn't demand we read or try to coerce us, but made it so inviting we rushed right in! I am indeed a grateful daughter. Thanks, Mom.

Ava Jamieson and Lorraine
Dinner dance at the club

10 "I have a fly down my ear" and other Lorraine stories

LORRAINE — KIRKUK, 1957/1958/1959

was lying in bed one night reading when I heard a fly buzzing around. I brushed it aside. Well, I must have brushed it just right because instead of going away from my ear it went down in my ear. Now, I thought, "Oh, I'm crazy." It was stomping around, and then it would buzz. It sounded like an airplane. It was definitely in my ear. I rolled over to the other side and pounded my head. Still there. Then I rolled back and lay very still, hoping it would crawl out. That didn't work either. Finally, I got up and telephoned the company medical center that we all called K-1 hospital. I told the head nurse what had happened. "I have a fly down my ear. Have you ever had that happen before?"

"Oh, yes, it has happened. Have Don bring you right down."

"He's not here. He's out on a drilling job. I don't know when he'll be back."

"Fine, I'll send a car for you."

I got dressed and went out to tell Hassan what was going on. He was sleeping. To wake him was like waking a dead person. I shook him awake, told him I was going down to the K-1 hospital, and if I wasn't home by the time the Sahb got home in the morning, to tell him where I was.

I start walking out the front door to wait for the car as an ambulance pulls up. Two men leap out, run for the back door, and grab a stretcher. "Put that thing back," I said. "I'll ride up in front."

The driver looked at me concerned. "Memsaab, you all right?"

"I'm fine."

In I climbed. A mile later: "Memsaab, you sure you all right?"

"There is nothing wrong with me except I have got a fly down my ear." By this time, I'm holding my hand cupped over my ear because I don't want that fly to get out. I hadn't been to the club. I hadn't had a drink. And I didn't want anyone to think I was crazy.

When we arrived, there's an orderly and a nurse waiting on the front stoop with a wheelchair to take me down this long corridor to the nurses' station. The British nurses were called sisters and wore big hats. The sister took some too warm water and flushed my ear. The third time, this little green fly floated out.

"You're lucky you came in," she said. "We had a man once that had a spider crawl down his ear, and he didn't come in. That thing died and festered in his ear. We had one heck of a mess." Now I could go home. They drove me back to the house in that same ambulance. I went back to bed and went to sleep.

In the morning, Hassan came to me and asked, "Memsaab, you go hospital last night?"

"Yes, I had a fly down my ear."

"A WHAT?!!!"

"A fly down my ear, but it's gone now."

Well, for the next two months, anytime I would lie in bed, I would swear they left a couple of legs in there because I'd hear this thing stomping around my ear. Finally, I went to the Irish doctor and told him my problem. "You have a look, because I just feel there's something still down there."

He looked and said, "No. It's all in your head, Lorraine. It's just your imagination."

Well, the story got around camp. It was one of the stories they loved to tell at the bar. People would come from other camps, and if I hadn't met them before, they'd say, "Oh, you're the one with the fly down her ear." I could have just died.

I always wanted to learn to eat with my fingers the Arab way. Ava, who was from Baghdad, offered to teach me. One morning, she called me and told me her husband, Bobby, had to go out of town and wouldn't be home for lunch. It would be a great time for her to show me how to eat the Arab way. She said, "I'll fix the food."

And I replied, "I'll be there." I laid out the midday meal for Don and the girls so Hassan could feed them when they arrived and raced over to Ava's. We went in the dining room, where there were just plates of food on the table, no silverware. She began to show me how to eat. The best way I can describe it is that you scoop up the food in curved fingers, and then with your thumb, you push it into your mouth. We're sitting there, and we're giggling, and we're laughing and having so much fun that we didn't hear the front door open.

"*What* are you two doing?!" It was Bobby. His trip had been canceled, and there he stood in the dining room door. Well, we couldn't deny it — we didn't have any silverware on the table. He thought we were disgusting. But we were having such fun! It was a good lesson. I learned something. I don't need silverware anymore to eat.

It was here in Iraq that I decided to never say I speak English. I would say I speak American. We had so many funny things happen with languages. Because we spent so much time with the British, our language differences were really highlighted. I'll never forget the night we were up at the club and one of my close married friends turned around and said to a bachelor who was leaving, "Knock me up at seven in the morning."

Well, I was shocked. "MAUREEN, what are you saying?"

"What do you mean?" she asked, a bit confused.

"We don't make appointments to do *that* in my country." Come to find out "knock me up" meant "ring me up." She wanted him to telephone her because they were going to play tennis in the morning.

Another time there was a very proper English lady, real so-phisticated looking, who turned to another bachelor with whom she had been playing bridge and said, "You sure diddled me last night." Well, I almost fell off the barstool. Turns out she was accusing him of winning through questionable means.

I remember visiting at a friend's house in England, hav-ing been invited for dinner. There were a number of guests at the table, and they were passing more food around. "Oh, I just couldn't," I remarked. "I'm so stuffed." Dead silence ensued while everyone turned to look at me. I whispered to the hostess, "Okay. What did I just do?"

Maureen smiled. "Well, we don't say we are stuffed in England — unless of course, we *are* pregnant, my dear."

ST. GEORGE'S TRON, GLASGOW, SCOTLAND

Rarely did I go to Scotland for business. But this one time I had developed two meetings with Glasgow-based companies — one a bank; the other, First Milk, a dairy group. This was a delightful happenstance because Glasgow was where Ava lived. Ava was for-ever complaining that I did not visit often enough, even though I managed to get there at least twice a year while at DreamWorks. This trip afforded a wonderful opportunity for a weekend together.

I could see why my mom and Ava were fast friends. Mom had a great sense of humor and could take a joke and laugh alongside you. Mom was also playful. Ava loved to tell the story of Bobby, my mom, and the dressing gown. She would kill herself laughing whenever she recounted it.

My husband, Bobby, was ill in hospital for a few days. He had this ratty, tatty, decrepit dressin' gown, given to him by an old girlfriend . . . that he couldn't bear to part with. I went into town and bought him a new dressin' gown to wear in the hospital. When I took it down there, he didn't want it. Bobby just wanted his old one. I was so embarrassed. I thought, "My God, he'll be wearin' that tatty dressin' gown forever."

I was tellin' Lorraine he was insistin' on his old gown when she said, "It's all right, dear. Don't worry about it. Just give it to me and I will send it to him." The next day, Bobby received a parcel. It contained his dressin' gown as Lorraine promised, packed in a big shoebox and sent special delivery to Bobby Jamieson at the K-1 hospital. When he opened it, he discovered his favorite dressing gown chopped up in little tiny pieces. Poor Bobby. He was brokenhearted. I was absolutely delighted. At long last we were rid of that ratty thing. I'll never forget his face when he spoke to me about the package. Bobby was seethin' as he told me how, when he got out of that hospital, he was going to kill me and kill Lorraine — both of us at the same time!

They were loads of fun but different. Ava was flashier than Mom. Ava loved to be the center of attention. One time when she visited California, I bought Ava a pair of rhinestone and gold tennis shoes. She insisted on wearing them out of the store and danced her way down Main Street in the little seaside town of Seal Beach. She was in her seventies at the time.

I can still picture Ava visiting our house in Garden Grove as President George W. Bush launched the military's shock and awe campaign, the bombing of Baghdad. The two old friends were sitting in the den, watching the television with tears streaming down their faces — Ava for her sister and many family members still in Baghdad, Mom for Ava's pain watching the destruction of the place of Ava's birth and the peril of her family still there. That was the wonderful thing about Mom. You could not only laugh with her, but you could cry as well. Mom was your friend through thick and thin.

On this visit, it wasn't long before the dressing gown story re-appeared. I heard again what a wonderful mother I'd had and all the fun they shared. Ava never tired of talking about their exploits in Iraq. Ava and Bobby's time in Kirkuk overlapped my family's time there for only about nineteen months, yet they still became fast friends for life. To listen to Ava, you would almost believe she missed Mom more than I did.

Ava lived in the sleepy wooded suburb of Newton Mearns and delighted in going into town to visit the shops. After a sausage (another fave) and egg breakfast, we boarded a bus that crossed the river Clyde and dropped us at Glasgow Central train station. The main shopping road was Buchanan Street nearby. I'm not much of a shopper but always enjoyed the walks and discovering so many different items. Sometimes we visited a department store called House of Fraser or the shops in Princes Square. Boots was almost always on the list because I was usually in need of some drugstore item or other — contact lens solution, face cream, a blister remedy, shampoo. Most of the time, we were on the hunt for a tea place, because I just had to have my tea and scones with clotted cream and strawberry jam. Honestly, I have so many favorites.

This trip, Ava had a special surprise. She was well aware of my passion for the pioneering designs of architect Frank Lloyd Wright — I had numerous books at my home. She wanted me to see the works of Glasgow's famed turn-of-the-century art nouveau design-er Charles Rennie Mackintosh. In 1903, he designed a tea shop in Glasgow called the Willow Tea Rooms that is a landmark to this day. It was here Ava had determined we would have tea on this outing. I was delighted by it all and bought a lovely pair of Mack-intosh-designed earrings for my sister Donna.

As we left, I could see the spire of a church just up the road. I wanted to visit it. We'd just about killed ourselves laughing this visit, which made me think of how playful and full of good humor my mom was. I didn't always see that growing up, but I did when Mom was viewed through Ava's lens. I was a somewhat humorless teenager who found little fun in being teased. Mom tried to help me to understand how important it was to learn to laugh at oneself or be the butt of a joke. "It goes away," she'd explain, "when one laughs. It lasts so much longer when you are sensitive and carry the hurt with you." It took a long time for me to get this lesson.

When we arrived at the church, St. George's Tron, we went in. I insisted on sitting apart from Ava because she would fill all the silences with her observations of life. She was a bit perplexed. Ava knew of my candle-lighting tradition, having been with me many times when I would light a candle for my mother. But there were no candles here. I told her it was okay. I didn't need a candle to do my thing. The minimalist interior was ever so vaguely reminiscent (I am almost afraid to make this comparison for fear of committing some grave offense) of Frank Lloyd Wright's Unity Temple interior. It was nice to have such a calm, clean space to let Mom know I finally got her point. I now have many laughs with friends and acquaintances at my own expense. I have that fun, playful side of Mom to thank for it.

Barbara goes to boarding school
in Lebanon

11 "Bring her home"

Barbara was the first to go to boarding school. My parents wanted to keep her as close as possible, so she ended up at a new school for Westerners in Beirut, Lebanon. Being in Lebanon meant she would be separated from the family for only a couple of months at a time, since she would be close enough to fly home for the holidays.

The thing about the Middle East is that it never seems stable for long. There were skirmishes that happened on a regular basis. Egypt's Gamal Abdel Nasser was tireless in his efforts toward Arab unity, modernization of his country, and anti-imperialism. He wanted to see all Arab nations allied against the West.

Lebanon in early 1956 experienced mounting internal pressures, as well as pressure from Egypt, due to its pro-Western stance. Christian president Camille Chamoun would not break diplomatic relations with the Western powers that had attacked Egypt during the Suez Crisis. By 1958, tensions had only increased. Lebanon was threatened by a civil war between Maronite Christians and Muslims. Barbara's school term ran October 8, 1957, to July 29, 1958, and near the end of term, she would end up in the thick of it.

LORRAINE — KIRKUK, 1957/1958

We had been in Iraq about ten days before school started Sunday, January 6, for all but Pam. The girls went to school on Saturday and Sunday and had Thursday and Friday off, the Iraqi holidays. I went with them the first day because the school was quite far from our compound in Kirkuk town. After the first month, I wrote about the school to my girlfriends back in the States.

The girls go to the company school. Boy is it advanced. Barbara (8yrs) is writing (English style) and knows her tables through the 10s. Has had a list of 478 spelling words since we arrived. Also pence and shillings, ft. in. yds. Boy has she worked. Kathy (6yrs) is on her 5s tables. Deedee (7yrs) — well I really don't know! School is so very hard for her. She needs to learn her tables through 7s. She's writing too. They are picked up by the bus at 7:30 A.M. Home for lunch 12:15 to 12:45. Home again at 4:45 P.M. But about three hours is spent on the bus. Piles of homework every night. The teachers are all English. After next week, the girls will be the only Americans in the school. There are four others now, but they have been transferred to Basrah. The other children are English, French and Dutch.

It was amazing to me the progress they had made by June, just six short months. In a letter to my close friend Margie, back in Lakewood, I recounted the progress.

We find to our amazement that Kathy is a natural learner. She learned her tables of 6 in about 5 min. Don wouldn't believe it, but he couldn't stump her — try as he did. She's the top of her class. We asked them to please not put her ahead this year as she would be in Deedee's room. We are so proud of the progress the girls have made here. Barbara has gone from the bottom of her class to the top too. And Deedee — well she can read real well now. Never thought she'd learn! And she's doing very well. She is the only one who gets really homesick for America. She wants to go home and live with you when she has to go away to school, she informed us.
Wow, the English accent they are developing. We

can lose Kathy in England anytime now. They are all picking it up, but it is only natural — cause they are the only American children here. Their teachers are all English too, so all new words have an English accent. It just kills Don. Haha.

I'll never forget the day it dawned on me. Deedee had been out playing with a little girl she knew when the streetlights in camp came on — their signal to come home. This night, Deedee came running in. "Oh, Mummy, I'm so sorry, I didn't see the lights come on. I'm sorry I'm late, but I was having such a smashing time at Jennifer's, I didn't notice."

I thought, "Wow, that one's gone." You could have taken the girls, put them in England, and thought they were British by this time.

From January until the end of term, July 29, Barbara remained with her sisters at the company school in camp. Unfortunately, she was in the final year of schooling that the company offered, and in October, we would have to find another place for her. The worst part of being overseas, as far as Don and I were concerned, was when the time came that we had to send the girls away to boarding school.

We were looking for a more local place to send Barbara. We didn't want to send her far away alone. I checked schools in Baghdad. There was only one possibility there, run by French nuns. It was down an alleyway with all these high brick walls around it and a wooden door with handmade lace curtains in the windows. It turned out to be the gloomiest place. It was just terrible. I could not have left her there.

When we were on a local leave in June, Don, Pammy, and I went to Beirut, Lebanon. The other girls stayed with friends so they would not miss school. We decided to check out the British Lebanese Training College, a place we had heard about, run by two Swiss sisters. They only had Arab students, but for the first time, the college was going to create a class for about twenty girls taught in English because of the demand from families living in the Middle East. If based in Lebanon, Barbara could come home for Easter and Christmas holidays, and I could see her sometimes in between. It had great appeal for us. When we went to the college, we liked it and the staff, so we thought, "We'll give it a try."

I fell in love with Lebanon on that leave. Beirut was quite cosmopolitan and often referred to as the Paris of the Middle East. It was under French rule from the 1920s to the 1940s, so both Arabic and French were spoken there. I couldn't believe the fresh fruits and vegs. In Kirkuk, we had a few in the winter, none in the summer. I ate shrimp, green salads, and the biggest strawberries I have ever seen with fresh whipped cream until they came out my ears. And the flowers! Wow! The Mediterranean Sea is the most gorgeous color. One night, sitting on the little balcony outside our room — it was so beautiful with the stars and moon sparkling on that exquisite body of water — I felt it was the most spectacular sight I had ever seen. Made me wish I was a writer, poet, or painter. I had to keep pinching myself to be sure it was still ME!

The summer holidays began shortly after we returned, and the broiling summer days were spent by the pool and enjoying camp life. By the time school resumed, the girls were all accomplished swimmers. In September, Deedee and Kathy returned to the company school, but Pammy was still too young. This gave me a couple of weeks with Barbara to prepare her for her new adventure in boarding school.

I'll never forget taking Barbara to the school. We flew in the company's eight-seater Dove plane which just happened to be going to Tripoli, Lebanon, first. The pilot and copilot were friends of ours. Ted angled the plane down low as we flew over the salt flats and the beautiful Mediterranean. It was one of the most delightful plane rides I have ever had.

We spent ten days in Lebanon between Tripoli and Beirut. When we arrived in Beirut, we checked into the Phoenician

Hotel. During one of our short holidays in Lebanon, Don and I had been to the mountains famed for the cedars of Lebanon. They were gorgeous. I decided to take Barbara up to Beiteddine to see the president's summer palace and to Baalbek, with its colossal Roman ruins. As we drove into the mountains, all the hills were terraced, planted with various crops and orchards. We also stopped along the way at Jeita Grotto with its towering stalactite caves and underground river. Barbara loved history, and she expressed such joy at all the sights.

One night, we went down to the bar to have a drink before dinner. Barbara ordered a Shirley Temple, and this wonderful bartender said, "I'm going to make you some people that move." Barbara looked at him with disbelief as he took some straws, twisted them together, and created little straw people that rolled around the bar. She was delighted with the show. Although Barbara is the oldest, Deedee was born when she was only thirteen months old, so she has no memories without sisters. This became a special trip because we enjoyed some alone time, which is difficult to get when you have three younger sisters.

It was hard to leave my nine-year-old daughter, but I was comforted with the fact that she was fairly close by. She would be home again in ten weeks for the Christmas break. Plus, Barbara was faithful and wrote home every week. The letters helped.

Upon my return, I wrote to my friend Margie back in Lakewood about the experience and the effect Barbara's absence was having on the other girls, especially the older two.

Wednesday, October 16, 1957
I returned last Wednesday from taking Barbara to boarding school. We spent ten days in Lebanon — between Beirut and Tripoli. We had a wonderful time. Hired a nanny to watch the others, but Hassan did the cooking, and most everything else here. When I

got off the plane, Ava met me with the girls. Don was working. I could have died when I saw Pammy — she had taken scissors and cut all her hair in front and on top and had a black eye from a fall. She also used up all my creams, perfumes, etc. I could strangle her every time I think of that, they are like gold here and so hard to replace. My drawers were in a mess. She said she wouldn't be good if I left her, and being her father's daughter, she keeps her word!

We are having trouble with Deedee over Barbara's absence in boarding school. She cries herself to sleep every night wanting her sister. Last night, no tears so we are keeping our fingers crossed. She even burst into tears at school the second day we were gone, and we can't even mention Barbara's name around the house without even more tears. Deedee told Don the other night, when he was trying to quiet her, that she just wanted to go to school where Barbara was. Don explained that next year she would, but that this year she still had other sisters and us and what was she going to do when she was away from home next year. She said, "I'll just probably cry for you and mummy and the other girls. I guess I'm just going to spend my life crying!"

Kathy says she doesn't cry but feels so sad inside that she just won't be able to laugh again till Barbara comes home. They make this so easy! I didn't realize how much this would affect them. But they really like each other and are very close.

After Barbara had been home for the Christmas holiday, I wrote again to Margie.

Wednesday, February 23, 1958
Don never says anything about missing Barbara

but I wish you could have watched his face while she was here. That one has a very special place in his heart. He even gained a few pounds.

Deedee is much better since Christmas. We've only had a few crying sessions. She's moved into Barb's bed though, and just counts the days until Barbara will be home. The whole holiday, poor Barbara couldn't move without Deedee right there. Barbara doesn't show affection easily and Deedee was always throwing her arms around her and kissing her and saying, "Oh, Barbara, I'm so glad you are home." And the three older ones jabbered away all the time. Barbara telling them all about her life at school, etc. I'm so glad they do like each other."

I received a letter from Barbara one day toward the end of her school term in late June. In it, she described how soldiers had been in the schoolyard because they thought there was a bomb in the tree. When they shot it down, it turned out the bag contained a sandwich. The Middle East was always having some sort of political unrest, and I supposed we were pretty used to it. But this was close enough for me. I did not like it. I called transportation and inquired, "When's the next plane to Beirut?" It was not for a couple of days. I said, "I want Barbara on it. Bring her home."

Then I called the school and told them to have her ready to meet this plane. They made plans to take her to the airport. It was quite risky to get an American child through the streets of Lebanon, where there was political unrest and abrupt outbreaks of violence. Barbara was instructed to lie down on the floor of a taxi, and a teacher was sent with her. This teacher told her if anybody stopped them and spoke to her, she was only to speak French and the teacher would answer. Fortunately, she knew a few words of French and did exactly as she was told. They got her to the airport all right, no problem, where she boarded the company plane and came home. Well, it was a few weeks later when the U.S. Marines moved in to stabilize Lebanon. We were packing for our leave so got her home just in time.

HEILIGGEISTKIRCHE — CHURCH OF THE HOLY SPIRIT, HEIDELBERG, GERMANY

Perhaps my parents had brought Barbara home just in time but for an additional reason. Barbara hadn't been home a month when the revolution in Iraq happened, and no Marines landed in Baghdad as they did in Lebanon to save the day. But at least for now, we were all together, unaware of what was to come, busily packing for our big four-month leave that would see us travel all over Europe and back to the States.

This was the happy yet active house Barbara came home to, secure with her family, swimming at the club with her sisters, pleased to be together once again. One realizes the value of family (and friendships) under such circumstances. My sisters and I are particularly close. We did not grow up with aunts, uncles, and cousins nearby. We relied on one another. My sisters are my best friends, even though we have spent much time apart over the years.

I could feel lonely for my family during my travels if I let myself. I traveled one or two weeks a month. I was so fortunate to have welcoming friends in many countries. This was one of the best parts of my travel. I have friends internationally whom I saw more often than I did some of my friends back home.

Bryan and Susanne Irvine and their daughters are one such family. Bryan is Donna's godson and in the U.S. military. His mother, Phyllis, had known my mother since Phyllis was sixteen and was one of the women with whom Mom corresponded from Iraq. Bryan met and married a most engaging German woman, Susanne. I spent many weekends in their home near Heidelberg.

The first weekend I visited them shortly after starting at Dream-Works, Bryan drove 156 miles to Cologne to pick me up and drove the 156 miles back to Heidelberg just for me to spend two days before catching a train to Paris. (Five hours of driving! After that, I managed to find my own way to Heidelberg.)

In the course of my visits, we went sightseeing to Heidelberg Castle, the zoo, dinners out, but more importantly, I participated in ordinary family life. I watched their daughter Melissa play basketball while another daughter, Annabel, as a part of the cheerleading squad, rooted her on. I saw Melissa all dressed up for prom night in this fabulous dress Donna had sent, we watched movies curled up on the couch, ate home-cooked meals, went shopping in town — so many things I rarely did back home. I never had any children, so I treasured these moments. The Irvines included me as a part of their family when I was away from my own.

I learned the value and joy of finding family wherever I wander because I found incredibly welcoming communities outside of my hometown. On this visit with the Irvines, we were shopping in Heidelberg. Susanne was explaining to me that Heidelberg is so picturesque and intact because it was not the focus of Allied bombings in World War II. It was a university town, not an industrial center like Frankfurt. It is home to Heidelberg University, Germany's oldest and one of Europe's most respected institutions.

When we wandered into the village square in the old part of town, it was dominated by the Heiliggeistkirche, or the Church of the Holy Spirit. It is a Protestant church but was one that did have candles. Susanne knew of my candle-lighting tradition for Mom. She gave me some time alone to sit and reflect. My gratitude that day was centered on what an amazing job Mom did building our little family into one where my sisters and I truly enjoyed one another's company, and for showing us that family exists in multiple forms. It is not just found in the biological structures of our DNA, but in the families we create through love and friendship. Lighting my candle this day, I thanked Mom for the gift of family, and for her and Dad's example of what a welcoming place a loving family can be.

King Faisal II, in full military uniform, on a state visit to London, 1956
Getty Images

12 "Don left for Baghdad": The revolution, part 1

LORRAINE — BAGHDAD, 1958

Our lives changed, and certainly those of a lot of people, on July 14, 1958. Early in the morning, Don left for Baghdad to get travelers checks for our leave. He and his baby driller flew down on the company plane. A baby driller is the name the men on the rigs used to identify an apprentice, a driller-in-training. When they landed in Baghdad, the red carpet was rolled out to the king's plane. Persian carpets were laid out on the platform that held his throne chairs. As Don and his baby driller were leaving the airport in the cab, people were lining the streets, waving flags and yelling. "Boy," Don said, "the king is getting a good send-off today." His Iraqi baby driller said nothing.

Soon they were caught in a terrific traffic jam of cars and people moving slowly along. When they found themselves in front of the Sandebad Hotel, the baby driller saw the owner inside the gates. By this time, he knew what was going on. He said, "Come on, Don, I'll buy you a cup of coffee."

"No," Don replied. "I've got to get to the American Express office so I can catch the plane back to Kirkuk."

"No, no, no, Don. I've *got* to buy you a cup of coffee." And with that, he proceeded to drag Don from the cab. The owner of the Sandebad Hotel had the gates locked. He quickly unlocked those gates and pulled both guys in.

"Hey, what the — "

"Don, the king isn't getting a good send-off. There's been a revolution. The king is dead." Don was in a state of shock.

They went onto the patio behind the Sandebad Hotel to have a coffee and talk things over. There was a large brick wall dividing the patio of the Sandebad Hotel from the Semiramis Hotel. On that patio next door were two people also having coffee — our close friends Ava and Bobby Jamieson. They were going home to Scotland for good and had come to say good-bye to Ava's family in Baghdad. Bobby recognized Don's voice coming over the wall and said, "Listen, Ava, that's Don Newton over there."

"Oh, no, it isn't," Ava replied.

Bobby put his chair on top of the table and climbed up to see for himself. He leaned over the fence. "Hi, Don, what are you doing here?"

Don almost died. They talked over the fence because they couldn't get to each other. He explained he was going to go to the American embassy to try to get some papers, because he had to have something with his picture on it to get a car to get back to camp. By this time, Don knew he wouldn't be able to fly back, and in those days, you didn't travel within Iraq with your passport, so he had no passport. He needed something in case he was stopped.

There was an additional errand he came to Baghdad to do. Don brought with him an order of thirty-six golf balls for a friend at the Daura refinery about twelve miles (twenty kilometers) southwest of Baghdad that needed to be delivered. Within a day or two, he somehow managed to get a cab to the refinery and talked his way in. He saw his friend Brad and delivered the golf balls. Before Don left, he asked, "I can't get through to Lorraine. Can you try to get a message through to Kirkuk that I'm all right and I'll get home as soon as I can?" Brad said he would, and Don hightailed it back to the hotel.

Meanwhile, his baby driller was having a stroke that Don had left the hotel. Don returned and told him he's now going to the embassy, to which his baby driller argued, "You can't. You can't go out on the street!"

Don said, "I'm going to the embassy!" So he starts walking. He sees the prince regent's body hanging from a post, and they had cut off his private parts and stuffed them in his mouth. They believe however you go to your grave, I guess, is how you are going to live in the afterworld. Anyway, Don was so disgusted he didn't have his Minox camera, because this camera looked like a cigarette lighter and hardly anyone would have noticed him taking pictures. We would have made a fortune on those pictures.

When he got to the embassy, guards wouldn't let him in because he didn't have his American passport. Don told the guards, "I'm going in there. Now, anybody that thinks they are big enough to stop me, try it." Well, at 6'4" and he looked tough, they let him through. When he got inside, he said, "I need a picture on a piece of paper. I don't care what it looks like. My picture with some Arabic writing on the paper that says I'm going to Kirkuk." He had quite a time getting his picture made, and he had to go back the next day to pick up the papers that he needed.

While he was there, he saw a young blonde American girl trying to sew pieces of cloth together of what had been her dress now shredded into strips. He went over and was talking to her. It seems she was hitchhiking through the Middle East — a terrible idea even in the best of times — with this German fellow when they were picked up by the army outside of Baghdad. The soldiers then split her dress to see if she was a blonde all over. There she sat, trying to sew these strips together. Don pulled out his wallet and said, "Look, honey, you're not going to make it sewing those," and he gave her some money. "Send one of the Iraqi women out to buy you a dress because you are going to have to get on the first plane out of here." She didn't want to take the money, so he explained, "I have four daughters in Kirkuk, and if one of my daughters was in trouble, I hope somebody would do this for her." He never got that girl's name. I've often wondered what happened to her.

Nuri al-Said, who was the prime minister of Iraq, was an old man and very unpopular due to his close ties to the British and the West. When the revolution happened, he went into hiding. He was caught trying to escape dressed as a woman in an abaya, the black covering women wore. The mob caught him, killed him, desecrated his body, and hung him up for all to see. Don saw his body hanging while returning to the hotel. When he returned, he got a chair and leaned over the wall to talk to Bobby. "I'm going to have papers tomorrow, and I'm going to hire a car, and I'm going back to Kirkuk. Why don't you and Ava come with me?"

Bobby replied, "Are you crazy? Your baby driller's going — an Arab, an American, a Scotsman, and one Iraqi woman? They'll kill us. We'd never get through." Bobby wouldn't leave the safety of the hotel, while Don remained determined to get home.

MEANWHILE, BACK IN KIRKUK . . .

"I'm not going": The revolution, part 2

LORRAINE — KIRKUK, 1958

On the same day Don left for Baghdad, July 14, I had an appointment at the American consulate in Kirkuk town. All four girls were on my passport. I wanted each of them to have their own passports because when we went on leave, Barbara and Deedee were to remain to attend school in England. Don and I didn't feel it was fair to have to teach them the Calvert system. It was a very good home-schooling system, but around the kitchen table, twenty-four hours a day, with your mother teaching you . . . well, we just didn't think it was the right way to raise our girls. Therefore, we made the gut-wrenching decision to send them to boarding school. We were condemned by most of the Americans for our actions. But the British applauded us because that's what they all did.

I entered the American consulate to resolve my passport issue, and they were in a state of shock. "What *are* you doing here? There's been a revolution in Baghdad."

I waved it off. "Oh, don't be silly. Don went to Baghdad this morning to get some money for our leave."

The assistant consul warned me, "Lorraine, get out of Kirkuk town!"

"Well, I have to go buy the girls some shoes."

To which he admonished, "You'd better get out of town." And they also claimed they couldn't do anything about my passport issue under the circumstances. That was a bit annoying.

I got back in the car, told the driver to take us to the

shoe place. We went in and I bought the girls shoes. Afterwards, I thought I'd stop at the grocery store I liked, then go down to the souk and buy some food on our way home. I got to the store, and the man there was in a state of shock too. "Oh, Memsaab, what are you doing here?" I told him what I was doing and that I was going into the souk. "Oh, no, madame. You cannot go into the souk."

"Look, everybody in Kirkuk knows me. Nobody is going to hurt me going into the souk."

"Get in your car and go home," he implored. "If you need any groceries, you call me, and I will bring them to camp for you. There are strangers in town that don't know you. They came in last night. We don't know where they are from. They don't know you, and I don't think you would be safe."

"Okay. I'll take your word for it. I'll go home." I went out and got in the car with the girls. Two young men came down the street and spat at the car. It was the first and only time I was ever spat at in Iraq. I had never seen them before, and I'm sure they were not from Kirkuk.

When I got home that day, all hell broke loose. The drilling superintendent called, "Where's Don?"

"Bill, you know he went to Baghdad this morning."

"Well, there's been a revolution."

"I know that now. You know that now. But Don didn't know that when he left to get money for our leave."

"Have you heard from him?"

"No, I haven't."

"Well, he'd better get back here."

And I replied, "I hope he does."

My phone started ringing practically nonstop. The personnel manager, the assistant manager of the company, the manager of the company. Everybody wanting to know if I knew anything about Don and who was with him and what was going on. I didn't know anything, but it sure made me nervous.

The next day, the phone continued ringing, so I wanted to get the girls up to the pool. I said to them, "Look, if you walk up to the pool and stay in the shallow end, I'll make some sandwiches, come up, and we'll have lunch up there." There was no lifeguard. If you had a nanny, they could go and supervise the children at the pool. If you had a houseboy, he wasn't allowed to.

I was in the kitchen making sandwiches when the phone rang again. I answered. A man said, "Mrs. Newton, you will be put under house arrest at one." It was about 12:30.

"What does that mean?"

"You have to have everyone in your house and stay in it," he explained. "The soldiers are coming into camp."

I turned to Hassan. "Hurry! Get on your bicycle and race up to the pool and tell the girls to come home now!" Immediately he raced up there. Of course, he grabbed Pam first — he had a little seat built on his bicycle for her.

He put her on there and told the other girls, "You walk. I come back." And down the driveway he rode with Pam on his bike. By this time, I am halfway up the driveway. I grab her and he goes back for Kathy. Then he goes back for Deedee and then Barbara. We got them all home in that half hour. House arrest descended on us like a dark cloud.

It was hot, of course, but we had air conditioning. Still, it's hard to keep four girls in the house all the time. I went out on the veranda just to see what was going on, and up from the hedge at the back of the garden came soldiers pointing rifles at me. I backed in the house real quick and stayed there.

The next day, the drilling superintendent calls again. "Where's Don?"

"I don't know. He's in Baghdad."

"Well, he's got to get back here!"

"Bill, can you get there?"

"No."

"Then how do you think he is going to get home?"

Then he proceeds to tell me, "Two Americans were mobbed and killed on the streets of Baghdad this morning. I want him back here."

Well, I grabbed that phone and called the manager. "Who were the two Americans mobbed and killed on the streets of Baghdad today, this morning?"

"How did you know? We didn't want you to know. We don't know who they are. We have no telephone communication with Baghdad. We don't know any more of what's going on than you do."

All I could see was Brad, who was 6'4" like Don, and my husband in Brad's little red Volkswagen with those damn golf balls being mobbed by Arabs and killed. At this point, I'm getting very nervous and called Dr. Tweedy, an Irishman. "Look, I'm getting a little bit nervous here. Having these four kids in the house all day under house arrest and all these phone calls. Send me something to calm my nerves." He did. Pronto. He sent it out by car.

About that time, another car shows up, and two teachers, June Ambrosek and Eileen, got out. Naturally, the girls were thrilled their teachers came to see them, and their angelic halos went up, believe me. They were so nice because they were worried about me and how I was doing. Asking if there was anything they could do. I really appreciated it.

The American assistant consul came by and told me there was going to be a plane coming as soon as they could arrange it to evacuate people. "Where to?" I asked. He said they were going to evacuate to Rome. I said, "I'm not going. What am I going to do in Rome?" Don had the checkbook in Baghdad, I didn't have enough money, and I didn't speak Italian.

He argued, "You must leave. It's not safe for you here. You have more American children than anyone in Iraq, and you have to be on that plane."

"If you think I'm going to be on that plane out of here without knowing if my husband is dead or alive, you're crazy. I'm *not* going." I'm sure he thought I was the crazy one.

It was the third or fourth night when the oil phone rang at about nine in the evening. We had two phones in the house. One was for local calls. One was an oil phone that connected company operations. An Iraqi voice said, "Memsaab Newton?" I affirmed. "Sahb okay. Sahb okay."

"Who is this?"

"Memsaab Newton, Sahb okay. He okay." He hung up.

The next morning, I rang the general manager and told him Don was all right. I had gotten a message last night, and I told him what was said. He asked, "Where did the message come from?" I told him I had no idea. "How could a message get through to you when we can't get a message through?"

"It came on the oil line phone, and I think it was your refinery, but I'm not sure. Have you tried the oil line?" I don't really think they had until I suggested it.

Rumors were flying all over. We had a little cheap radio that would pick up local news. Hassan would listen and try to tell me what was going on. Hassan looked at me and said about the soldiers in camp, "Memsaab, you no worry. Hassan take care of you. Nobody hurt my Memsaab and chikos. Kill Hassan first."

With that, I went and got a pencil and paper and wrote down Don's sister's name, address, and telephone number. I said to Hassan, "If anything happens to me, you take the chikos into Kirkuk into a mud hut. You put abayas on them and tell them 'no speak.' And I will tell them no, they are not to speak. Hide them there until the trouble is over. Then look for an American flag. Take them to the American flag with this note and give it to them. They will take care of the children and see that they get back to America." I had him bring me one of his jackets. I took apart the shoulder pad and sewed the note inside. "Now you take care of this jacket, and be sure this jacket is the one you have with you."

The American assistant consul was at the house every

day, trying to get me to leave. One Pan American plane came in from Basrah, where they picked up women and children only. Then it went to Baghdad to do the same and on to Kirkuk. Don was still not home, and I still refused to go on that plane. Big planes like this one usually didn't land in Kirkuk. I'll never forget standing on my veranda, watching the Pan American World Airways plane gain altitude as it flew above my garden. I could read the PAA on the underwings of the plane as it passed over. I stood there and said a silent prayer, "Dear God, am I doing right? But I can't leave, but I don't want to endanger my children's lives." I just felt it wasn't right for me to leave.

Meanwhile, back in Baghdad . . .

Don and his baby driller managed to hire a car to bring them to Kirkuk. His baby driller insisted on going with Don. He wasn't about to let Don cross that desert alone. There were rumors of the sheik's army from the north marching south to Baghdad. There was also only one main road. Everybody thought they were crazy going to Kirkuk because they would encounter this army as they drove north.

Kirkuk was 150 miles north of Baghdad, and there were no freeways or good roads. It took a while, but they managed to get to Kirkuk town, no problem. They didn't see a soul going across the desert. He dropped his baby driller off in town and drove to the gates of the camp. The guards would not let him in. Don was within a half mile of the house, and no way would they open that gate and let him through.

He turned his car around and drove to the general manager's house. Don had gotten to know Angus, a great big Scotsman with a red beard, when he was stationed in Basrah before we arrived in Iraq. It was after midnight when he rang the doorbell and pounded on the door to wake the man up. Angus came to the door, surprised. "Don, what are you doing here? How did you get here?"

"I got a car and I came. I've got to get home to my family. I'll tell you one thing — I made it to the gate, and the guards and the army were there. They won't open that gate and let me through. Now either *you* get ahold of them and tell them to have that gate open by the time I return, or this car is going through it." He was so mad. Angus got on the phone, reached the army general, and when Don returned, the gates were open.

It was about two in the morning when we heard someone coming through the front door. I couldn't believe it; neither could Hassan because he was on alert in case something happened. But it was Don, coming home. I forget if he was gone five nights or six nights. In that moment, it didn't matter — was I ever glad to see him!

ST. MARGARET'S CHAPEL, EDINBURGH CASTLE, SCOTLAND

Mom was thirty-five when the revolution occurred. She had four children, five to ten years old . . . with a missing husband. I was amazed at how calmly she handled the situation. I had no idea she was nervous in any way. Indeed, I never knew until I listened to the recordings that she ever called one of the camp doctors for medication. Of course, my sisters and I saw the soldiers with guns, but I have no recollection of fear. It just was. Mom obviously worked hard to keep things as normal as possible and reassure us.

I thought it was brilliant of her to make a plan if anything should happen, to tell Hassan what to do. How did she come up with the idea to sew our aunt and uncle's address into the shoulder of his coat, show him an American flag, and then tell him to hide us until the fighting was over? I'm not sure Hassan would have been around to carry out her plan if someone tried to harm our mother. I have no doubt he would have given his life for her, or for any one of us, for that matter.

I have never had to face such a dangerous situation in my travels. There were concerns about terrorism in Europe, but at that time, those incidents were few and far between. I always felt if I had an accident, DreamWorks would take care of getting me home. I have great faith. Besides, I wasn't flying to any third world countries. My itinerary read like a travel brochure: Berlin, Munich, Cologne, Paris, London, Madrid, Sydney, Melbourne, Seoul, Hong Kong.

On this trip, I had taken the weekend to go and visit Mom's good friend Ava Jamieson in Glasgow again. We decided to go to Edinburgh to visit the shops on Princes Street (too touristy for me) and see Edinburgh Castle. It was common for our conversations to stray to Mom. Ava really missed her too. On the hour-long train ride, we talked about the revolution. It was funny because in recounting Dad's invite to join him on the drive back to Kirkuk, Ava said, "Being an American, he had to go back. Bobby and I, being frightened people, stayed behind until things cleared up. Then we went back up [to Kirkuk] by train before we left for good." Somehow, she was of the opinion that Americans were brave. I thought about that for a while and then concluded that I wholeheartedly agreed with her assessment.

In our walk around Edinburgh Castle, we visited St. Margaret's Chapel. I was surprised to learn it is the oldest surviving building in Edinburgh. It is such a sweet little place, tiny, with some seating along the narrow walls. I knew it would be hard to have a quiet moment with Ava in tow. She loved to talk. I convinced her to stay outside and enjoy a bit of sun since it was such a lovely day. "I'll only be a minute," I promised. I entered and stood as close to the roped-off altar as I could get. I spoke to that spirit of my mom that is always with me in my heart, saying, "You know, Mom, I really think Ava got it right. Americans are brave. Maybe not me so much but certainly you and Dad. Thank you for being so brave and keeping us safe. Because of you, I do not feel like 'frightened people.'"

Street demonstrators in Baghdad with posters in support of new military leader Karim Qasim
Getty Images

14 "A gloom kind of settled over the camp"

LORRAINE — KIRKUK, 1958

A gloom kind of settled over the camp. All of our activities weren't the way they had been; they were curtailed a great deal. We never knew when the phone would ring to tell us, "You're under house arrest in thirty minutes." If we were up at the pool, somebody would come out and announce, "Go home. You're under house arrest in thirty minutes." Rumors were flying that the army general Karim Qasim, who orchestrated the coup d'état, was in power. It seemed fairly quickly the fighting stopped, and things started to settle into an adjusted routine. Along with that, magazines began coming into the country again. Everybody was racing to buy *Time* magazine, except all the pages to do with the revolution and Iraq had been torn out. A couple of brave pilots smuggled in the torn-out pages. Those were passed all around camp so the adults would know something of what was going on. Our family and friends back in the States did not know what was happening with us and were worried. They felt validated when they told me I shouldn't take my girls to this heathen country. Now look what happened.

A few days after the revolution, the sweeper, the gardeners, and the trash people came back. When the sweeper and gardener came to our house, they just sat down on the veranda with their backs against the wall. Hassan goes shooting out there to find out "Why you no work! Go do your job!"

And the sweeper explained, "We don't have to work anymore. The company belongs to us. We don't need to do anything. They just give us money now."

Furious, Hassan bellowed, "Are you crazy? Nobody give you baksheesh for nothing!" They eventually got up and moved around a little.

You couldn't entertain like before because people never knew when they would be ordered into confinement. Even so, Don had a good friend, Philip Rhoades, who would come to our house for a meal quite often. Philip's family had gone back to England, so he was staying at one of the messes for the bachelor men. This one evening, he was late, which was odd because he was always so prompt. I called the mess to find out where he was. An Iraqi man answered and when I asked for Philip Rhoades, the man became evasive. Something strange was going on, and this man wouldn't tell me anything. I repeated, "Mr. Rhoades is due at my house for dinner. Is he there?"

"No, no, no" was the only reply he gave, and I just couldn't figure it out.

Don was also late home that night, and when he arrived, I told him about this curious exchange. Don had his truck, so he said, "I'll run over to the mess and see." When he came back, he told me that Philip had been taken out of there in handcuffs by the army. Nobody knew anything else. We had a gloomy dinner that night, and we worried because we didn't know why Philip had been taken into custody.

The next day, everyone in camp was called to be at the cinema at six o'clock in the evening. It was mandatory. So, of course, we all went. Angus Purse, our general manager, got up on the stage and said that everyone's letters were being censored in and out of the country: "Please be careful what you write." He went on to explain that one member of the community had written to his mother that the Arabs in a mob are like animals and was arrested. (*Any* mob is like animals, as far as I'm concerned.) Now we all knew what Philip had done. Then we found out the company had managed to "negotiate" to get Philip out of the country within twenty-four hours. Otherwise, I'm sure he would still be in that jail to this day, rotting there.

I think Ava and Bobby caught the second plane out of Iraq when service resumed. However, they had already quit before the revolution. Now people were quitting right and left and leaving because of the revolution. There was no way we wanted to quit. Not only did we have a big holiday coming up, but we felt hopeful things would sort themselves out and this interesting life could continue on.

I had spent a great deal of time with a travel agent in Kirkuk planning and booking our tour. I'd spoken with lots of people, asking for suggestions and recommendations for "do not miss" sights in the places where we were visiting. I'd "argued" with Don about the locations and money before settling on an itinerary that we both felt was workable. The company gave us round-trip, first-class airfare to our home city (Los Angeles, California) in cash. That cash is what we used to travel coach. It was how we were able to see and do all the things we did.

The tour plan included travel to Rome, Germany, Vienna (Austria), Brussels (Belgium), then on to England. We needed a few days to check out some boarding schools for Barbara and Deedee to attend that school year. We were booked across the ocean on the *Queen Mary*, then on to California and back to the U.K. on the *Queen Elizabeth*. Upon returning to England, we would take Barbara and Deedee to the boarding school we selected earlier. Afterwards, it was back to Iraq with just Kathy and Pam via Portugal, Spain, and a cruise on the Mediterranean that stopped in Egypt before setting us down in Beirut — a short hop away on the company plane back to Kirkuk. We were going to be gone for four months. We were overdue to go on our leave, and I was impatient to get under way. It was time.

ST. JAMES'S CHURCH, PICCADILLY, LONDON, ENGLAND

Of course, Mom was impatient to get under way. She was excited to behold all these wonders she had been reading about and hearing about and planning to see for the last year or so. The house was packed up, Hassan on loan, reservations made, and suitcases lined up at the front door. But she had one more thing she needed to do — get rolls of undeveloped film and other small items out of the country. One never knew what was going to happen or even if one would return.

It was during this first leave that our lives as world-class smugglers began. As Mom explained,

> *I took the girls' coats, filled up nylons with film and family things that might be confiscated. Then I pinned the nylons inside the coat sleeves. I told them not to set them down or jump around or anything and hold onto them until we got on the plane, which they did. This way we managed to get out everything that we wanted. Now, some of the British were afraid the sterling silver was going to be confiscated, so they tied a string around their waist under their clothes to move these valuables out through customs. They even tied their sterling silver napkin rings and the silver-plated cutlery to these hidden strings. They got out a lot of things. We women were very creative.*

You could be aghast that Mom would take a risk such as this, but she wasn't dealing drugs or doing anything immoral. And there were no metal detectors in those days. Only a pat-down search would have revealed this activity, and those were rarely done to foreign women.

Mom wanted to get rolls of film containing our family photos out of the country, along with a few things she treasured. Mom never took the sterling or anything that belonged to the company. Perhaps I feel comfortable with a measure of risk and uncertainty because of these early learnings. Calculated risks are a part of business, and I have always been willing to take some and manage the result, good or bad.

A colleague and I were in a meeting with the second-largest supermarket chain in the U.K., Sainsbury's, in early September. I had prepared some concepts for a promotional partnership that were creative but not beyond the bounds of these kinds of movie tie-ins. Shortly into the meeting, the commercial director of Sainsbury's, Paul, said, "I want to do something together that has never been done before. What can we do that's new and exciting?" After he rejected a couple more ad hoc ideas as not innovative enough, I remembered the rooftop concert Jeffrey Katzenberg, our CEO, had hosted for the employees of DreamWorks featuring Academy Award–winning composer Hans Zimmer. I thought, "Why not?" The concert was magical for me when I experienced it on that rooftop. Perhaps it could be magical for Sainsbury's customers as well. I pitched the concept not knowing if it was even possible or would be approved by the studio. Naturally, that was the idea that struck a chord with Paul. He wanted to create a day in the park a whole family could enjoy with the theme keyed to the release of *Kung Fu Panda 2*. The event would feature a live concert by the film's composers and activities for children sponsored by Sainsbury's suppliers.

Over the coming months, I made several more London trips, and Paul and I exchanged countless phone calls. A myriad of details had to be considered and issues resolved before we could determine if the event could be mounted to our satisfaction. The schedule had to be laid out, a budget created, and permissions secured from the studio; the in-demand composers, Hans Zimmer and John Powell, had to be available and willing to participate; legal approvals had to be obtained, clearances achieved, and vendor support garnered before the plan could be presented to the Sainsbury's board. In March, it was greenlit and I boarded a plane.

The event was to take place at the beginning of July — not enough time. Had either Paul or I realized the toll this would take, we might have pulled back. By this time, his wife was pregnant with their fourth child, and I still didn't have an assistant to support all the logistical elements the event would require. Yet neither one of us got where we were by shying away from a little work. It was a great concept; therefore, the event was set in motion.

The first meeting after the Go button had been pressed included more than twenty Sainsbury's folks and some key vendors. The venue had been confirmed: Althorp, the estate of the Spencer family and home to Lady Diana Spencer, later Princess of Wales. It is where she grew up and where she is buried on an island in a lake near the main house. At the meeting, an overview was presented. We all dispersed to our departments with much to do. I decided to walk back to my hotel. It gave me a chance to think and stretch my legs. I must admit, I enjoyed more than my fair share of nice days since it rarely rained on me when I traveled. My friends used to call me to ask when I was coming so they could plan their outdoor activities. It was quite funny how lucky I was.

There is a small courtyard up the road from my usual London hotel. I had passed it many times without realizing there was a church within. Piccadilly is such a major London thoroughfare, and this church blended into its surroundings so well that I missed it. Many days when I would pass by, there was a street market going on in the courtyard. Ever in a hurry, I did not stop to investigate until this day, when I was returning from the Sainsbury's meeting. I discovered a tranquil church amid the bustle of daily life. It was designed by Christopher Wren (as were many churches in London, including the iconic St. Paul's Cathedral). Delighted, I slipped into one of the wooden pews and reflected on my breathtaking day.

When I was a teenager, Mom accused me of being "a cockeyed optimist — just like your father!"

At the time, I replied, "It beats having a depressed daughter around all the time." Today I might respond, "Takes one to know one." Mom never let details stand in the way of getting where she wanted to go.

I believed what she always said: "Where there's a will, there's a way." Why she would give me a hard time about something I had confidence I could achieve was a surprise to me back then. She had faith she could figure things out. So did I. I realize today I am not just like my father. I am just like my mother. As I lit my candle in St. James's Church on Piccadilly, I thanked Mom for teaching me to be like her and say yes to the possibilities in this world. Tomorrow would be a great day to figure out how to make that "yes" from Sainsbury's happen.

Vienna
Kathy, Deedee, Lorraine (in arm cast), Pam, Miss Alice, Barbara

"Tales from the Vienna Woods": First leave, part 1

LORRAINE — HOME LEAVE, 1958: CONTINENTAL EUROPE

After the revolution, the first airline to go back to a normal schedule in an unstable country was Lufthansa. Don said after Lufthansa was brave enough to establish service under such precarious conditions that he would always fly Lufthansa in the future if they had a flight going his way. And he did, starting now.

Our itinerary had been loused up by the revolution and our late start, so we bypassed Rome and Geneva. We spent a few days in Munich, Germany. I remember there was a wonderful park that had an elephant ride. All the girls climbed aboard, except Barbara, who wasn't about to, and had their picture taken. Then we went to Vienna, where we stayed for eleven days.

When Don woke up from the first night in the low-budget Viennese hotel, he protested, "My God, this hotel must have been a hospital during World War II. That's the most damn uncomfortable bed I ever slept on in my life." Now, Don has been in some pretty rough situations, so that bed must have been something awful.

We set out to see the Anker clock (Ankeruhr) in Hoher Market square. Every hour, life-sized figures dressed in historical clothing move across the clock face. The friend who had recommended the stop made clear that the most important time to get here was at noon, when we would be able to see all twelve of them. At one or two o'clock all you would see is one or two figures. The chimes began. Each time the clock struck a note, a full-sized figure from way back in time would come around. The clock was suspended above us in the middle of an enclosed bridge that connected two buildings. It was most interesting.

While we were standing there, I noticed a woman in Viennese dress. She was holding a little dog, who had on a collar and tie. We started chatting. She spoke excellent English, having just returned from England. Her name was Miss Alice. Don was telling Miss Alice about the problem with our hotel, specifically his bed, and she asked, "How long do you have to stay?" He told her. She suggested, "Well, what you do is you go to the railroad station. You can find good lodging there much cheaper." This appealed to Don, especially the "much cheaper" part.

After leaving me and the girls at an outdoor café, Miss Alice and Don set off for the railroad station. We waited . . . and we waited . . . and we waited . . . and they finally came back. They had found the top floor of a house in the suburbs where we could stay. The couple's daughter was getting married, so they were renting out the top floor to earn money for her wedding. We moved there immediately with the help of Miss Alice. We spoke no German, and the lovely couple spoke no English, but we managed just fine.

The space was one big room with three feather beds and comfy eiderdowns. There was a kitchen and a bath. In the garden downstairs, there was a sweet little playhouse that fascinated the girls. Before Miss Alice left that day, we had hired her to take the children to the zoo and places they would enjoy, while Don and I did the things we wanted to do.

The next day, we stayed around the house in the morning to be sure our daughters felt comfortable with Miss Alice. Then Don took the girls out with Miss Alice in the afternoon while I stayed behind to do the wash and shop in the local markets nearby. On one road, there were two meat markets across the street from each other. One had a red front, the other a green front, both with signs I couldn't understand. I peeked in each one of them and then bought some hamburger and stew meat from the shop whose offerings looked the best. I was going to cook so we'd have some meals after our outings.

Don and Miss Alice had made arrangements for Don and me to visit the Vienna Woods and travel on the Blue Danube River. She'd helped him to work out the trolley system too. Before leaving the next day, I handed Miss Alice all the change I had, not knowing that Don had done the same. We headed off down the street to catch the trolley in time to make our tour. Once on board, the conductor came around. Don had no change for the fare. "Honey, give me some change."

"I don't have any. I gave all my change to Miss Alice."

"Well, so did I. That's all right," and he pulled out a bill. It was apparently too large, and the conductor wouldn't accept it. The conductor wanted us to get off at the next stop, but Don refused. Since Don was 6'4", the conductor didn't argue it. Further down the line, Don saw a bank. "You stay right here. I'll get this bill changed and be right back." The minute Don was off the trolley, the conductor physically lifted me from my seat and shoved me off onto the sidewalk. Don comes running out of the bank. "What did you get off the trolley for?"

"I didn't get off. He threw me off!"

"Well, you should have just sat there."

"I couldn't." What's the point in arguing? We were now in danger of missing our tour. A taxi stand just happened to be across the street, so we raced on over and made the tour just in time.

The Vienna Woods were wonderful. Tall, lacy trees that let the soft sunshine through, meadows of grasses and flowers, paths of fallen leaves, and stumps covered in moss. Such a majestic country. All that echoed through my head on that trip was the Strauss waltz "Tales from the Vienna Woods."

The next morning's boat tour of the Blue Danube failed to reach the heights of the day before. It was a disappointment. I expected the Danube to be a blue like the Mediterranean, and it certainly wasn't. The views of the city were quite lovely, though. I loved Vienna. There were statues on buildings, and just a trolley or taxi ride was such a thrill. It was an absolutely beautiful city. We continued on to the opera house and really wanted to visit the famous Spanish Riding School, but unfortunately, the horses were on tour in America at the time. Nobody said we could see the stables and the grounds and the other horses, so we missed it. I've always been sorry about that.

The next day, we set off as a family to visit the biggest Ferris wheel in the world. I wasn't going to get on it because I don't like heights, but I couldn't miss this so I stepped aboard. It was like getting on an enormous elevator and going around. We all enjoyed the views. The city also had these immense swings. You stood up on them and made them fly by bending your knees and leaning back. A similar experience to the seated ones found in playgrounds back home, only these were really tall. Deedee, especially, loved to swing and delighted in riding hers as high as she could make it go.

By this time, I had learned a few polite words in German such as *auf wiedersehen, danke schön, guten Morgen*, and had become a familiar sight down on the little shopping street. One morning, I was at the shops and met our landlady. She fell in step with me, and we would point at things in the shop windows, nodding to each other. We couldn't talk, so we smiled a lot as we walked along. When the landlady headed into a meat shop, I placed my hand on her arm, directing her attention to the meat shop across the street. The landlady shook her head. *"Nein, nein, nein."* I couldn't understand why not and again indicated my desire to go to the meat shop across the street. At that moment, a policeman was passing by on a horse. The landlady pointed at the horse, clopped a little bit to make me understand the meat on the other side of the street was horse meat. I had been feeding my family horse meat! I giggled to myself all the way home, but I never told Don or the girls at that time because I didn't know how they would take it. Kathy was horse crazy and probably would not have forgiven me this transgression at seven years of age.

I had heard about a restaurant down in the old university quarter on Fleischmarkt Street, where Mozart, Wagner, Beethoven, Mark Twain, and Shakespeare had all eaten and signed one of the walls. Well, this I just had to see! We asked Miss Alice to babysit one evening while we ventured out to this historic restaurant. After we left the trolley, we walked until we saw what I had been told to look for, a life-sized black iron figure above a restaurant sign. The restaurant was called Griechenbeisl ("Tavern of the Greeks"). I was told it was the oldest restaurant in Vienna, dating from the 1400s, and a most well-regarded place to dine. Don and I each ordered steak and battered deep-fried mushrooms. I think that was the best meal I ever had in Europe!

When we left the restaurant that night, I wanted to be sure I'd remember the sign. The sidewalk was wide, and I didn't realize it narrowed. I was backing up, looking up to see the sign, and I tumbled off the curb, using my right hand to break the fall. The next day, my wrist was hurting, so Miss Alice insisted I go to the hospital. The X-ray showed it was broken. I was led into another room. It was cold, I was seated on a wooden slat bench, and a big black apron was placed over me. Nearby was a trough with plaster, and they put a cast on my arm from my hand past my elbow, placed it in a sling, and back to the house I went.

Traveling had already been a challenge on this trip because we had a lot of luggage. Being gone for four months required us to carry both summer and winter clothing. (Plus, we were leaving Barbara and Deedee in boarding school for a year.) Even though I washed clothes at various stops, that's a lot of clothes for six people. Whenever we moved from city to city — or moved hotels within a city — it required two cabs. Don would ride in one with all the luggage, and I would follow behind with all the children. Now my family had an added burden, a mother with her right arm in a sling, making it all the more difficult. Barbara and Deedee helped me take a bath, and the girls were very good helping where they could. But I just couldn't believe this had happened just when we were due to depart for Brussels and the World's Fair.

A couple of days later, we boarded a plane, me in a sling and cast, and flew to Brussels. After the revolution loused up our travel plans, we were finally back on track and arrived on the date we were due, according to the slip of paper from the travel agent with the confirmed reservation written on it. Yet the hotel had never heard of the Newton family and had no rooms left. We weren't just staying a night or two in each city. We had arranged to stay from several days to a week or more, so we would have plenty of time to see everything. When our reservations weren't set, it was quite a problem. This very kind manager felt so sorry for us, he called around and found us a place for the night. Then he managed to get us in some government housing that had been put up for the World's Fair for the remainder of our stay.

I certainly wasn't going to let my arm stand in the way of seeing the World's Fair! The next day, we put the girls in a nursery on the fairgrounds, while we went off to get the lay of the land, to scope out the expo before bringing the children with us. The World's Fair contained a variety of exhibitions by various nations in uniquely designed pavilions. It was dominated by a polished aluminum multisphered structure that was about as tall as the Statue of Liberty or Big Ben. It looked a bit like an atom, hence the name Atomium, containing eight exhibition spheres soaring around the core.

Of course, we went to the American pavilion straight away. There was a huge line that snaked away from the entrance. Don asked the guard how long the wait was and was told two to three hours. Don explained that we had four children in the nursery and couldn't wait that long, guess we were just going to have to miss it. The guard motioned us around the corner of the building and placed me with my broken wrist in a wheelchair. Pushing me to a special entrance, Don and I enjoyed the next showing, with me sitting comfortably, while everyone else was standing. Afterwards, the guard pushed me back outside again, so we could continue exploring. It was fun. We spent several days at the expo with the girls before moving on to the sights of the city. Interestingly, the American pavilion found a home after the World's Fair ended at Disneyland in California. We visited it there too when we returned home to California in 1962.

In my reading about Brussels, I learned about a boy statue that waters this fountain with his little doohickey. Every week, they changed his clothes, all tailored just for him. Well, you know, I just had to see that! While we were walking down the street, we passed beautiful flower stalls, open-air markets with all sorts of things, and food vendors. One was selling French fries in newspaper like they sold fish and chips in England. The vendor put a glob of mayonnaise on top and handed it over. It was so good, and to this day, both Deedee and Pam have mayonnaise with their French fries.

Next stop after Brussels was Amsterdam, Holland (the Netherlands). By this time, Don was an experienced traveler. He went to the railroad station and found us accommodations in a private home willing to accept six of us. The owner's daughter kindly offered to wash and iron our clothes. I was grateful, as we had a flock of dirty dresses* . . . again!

Our first stop was Volendam (a city about thirty minutes outside of Amsterdam), where they make Edam cheese.

---

* By the way, Mom always wore dresses, and so did "her girls." I never saw my mom in trousers until I was a teenager.

The city was right on the Zuider Zee, a shallow bay only about fifteen feet deep, connected to the North Sea that was closed off in the 1930s to form a large lake. On our way we passed windmills, narrow drainage canals running through the farmlands, and a very flat landscape for as far as the eye could see. No mountains and no wooden shoes. The girls were very disappointed because they thought everyone in Holland wore wooden shoes.

In Volendam, we heard of a little island called Marken with very picturesque wooden houses, no cars, just carts with donkeys, and the people wore the traditional dress of Holland. Today it is connected to the mainland, but back then we had to take a boat over. It is here that Don took one of my favorite pictures, Deedee sitting next to a little Dutch girl in full folk attire and clogs, as the wooden shoes are known as in Holland. The little Dutch girl is staring at Deedee with such an indignant look on her face. Back in Volendam, there was a dress-up shop, so I had a picture taken of all of the girls in traditional costume, complete with clogs.

We went to museums, palaces, and artists' houses, not just here but in all the cities we visited. We saw a lot. Amsterdam was built on canals. The houses that lined the waterways were skinny and five or six stories tall, which just made them appear narrower. The girls remarked that they had never seen so many bridges and bikes. We all thought Holland was lovely, yet very different than any city we had ever seen before.

The only thing I didn't experience in Holland that I wanted to was the diamond factory. I knew people who had purchased diamonds there. By this time, I could have bought out all of Europe, and Don had adopted the saying "We came to see, not to buy." I could choke on those words to this day! Another one of Don's oft-repeated phrases when that glint came in my eye as I looked at jewelry: "I gave you four little jewels. Why would you want more?" We finally came to an agreement. Every time we had a leave, he would buy me one piece of jewelry. Now, my tastes are not inexpensive, but I didn't feel I could go real high. After all, I did have those four little jewels.

ST. JAKOB (ST. JAMES THE GREATER), NUREMBERG, GERMANY

I am in awe of my mother and her diligence in preparing for our leave. The efforts behind logistics can never be underestimated. In my world, not only would I have to create individual pitches for each meeting but also spend a fair amount of time planning the in-country travel. I had to know the location and travel route; my modes of transport, which were usually trains and the underground/metro; and what kind of connections would be required for each appointment. The process could be tedious, involving transportation schedules and walking or taxi time with maps to show the way. I was fortunate not to have to go through this process in most countries as I was usually with our agents, but I did take many meetings alone in the U.K. and some in France. Even more challenging, the availability of my company's potential business partners varied, causing numerous changes to the schedule and travel as my agent and I worked to fit appointments in on the one, two, or three days that I was in a particular country. Travel was a logistics puzzle that took a lot of time, either by me or especially by our agents.

There were two trips each year where filling a schedule at the convenience of our partners was no problem. They were all in one place, and indeed one could hardly fit in all the meetings. One trip was to Brand Licensing Europe, a trade show held in London every October. All the companies that had characters or people to license — such as the entertainment studios, publishers, artists, celebrities, music bands, and gaming companies — could meet with manufacturers, retailers, and consumer brands who were looking for licensing opportunities and partnerships. The other was Spielwarenmesse — Nuremberg International Toy Fair in Germany — the largest toy fair in the world, held each year in late January – early February. Seventy-three thousand people attend from over 120 countries to view almost three thousand exhibitors' toys and games.

The first time I attended Nuremberg Toy Fair, my going was decided too late for me to book a hotel room in the city. The closest hotels were booked a year in advance, so I commuted each day from Munich. It's around a hundred miles and would take about an hour each way on the high-speed ICE train. One evening, I took a taxi into the old walled city of Nuremberg to have dinner with a Dream-Works toy partner. I had an hour to kill, so I chose to walk around this historic town. I discovered St. Jakob (St. James the Greater), a medieval church heavily damaged during World War II, as were many of the churches in Germany. Even though it had been rebuilt, it maintained its antique and gloomy feel.

It was late in the day, already growing dark as it was the beginning of February, still winter. A slight flurry of snow began to swirl as I entered the church. I sat quietly. Thoughts of my mom and dad traveling for four months, *four months*, with all that luggage and us girls overwhelmed me. Other than the initial trip over and her visits to Lebanon, Mom had done little traveling and certainly nothing on that scale. The complexity of it all simply amazed me. Just thinking about it is daunting to me. But it never was to Mom, no, not to her. It was a massive opportunity for adventure and to fulfill her dreams of seeing the world. I was grateful for Mom's master planning capabilities. This twilight afternoon as I lit my candle, I was thankful to Mom for making the most of it and taking us all along for the ride.

Pam and Lorraine
Car loaded with luggage in the U.K.

16 "Traveling with Father was something" First leave, part 2

LORRAINE — HOME LEAVE, 1958: ENGLAND

Nothing had gone as planned on the trip thus far, so the first day in London, Don said, "I'm going down to the Cunard Line and be sure our reservations are all right." Well, he came back to the hotel madder than an ox! The Cunard Line had never heard of the Newton family, had no reservations on either the *Queen Mary* or the *Queen Elizabeth*, and they were sold out. Was I going to have a word with that travel agent when we returned!

We had two key reasons for being in England. One was for us to attend the yearly IPC company ball, and the other was to interview headmistresses at the boarding schools I had written to prior to our departure from Iraq. I was very disappointed to learn that my first choice, a school in Edinburgh, Scotland, had room for only one girl. We would never ever separate Barbara and Deedee.

Don rented a car, and we headed over to see the school in Ascot, famed location of Britain's most prestigious horse race. Whenever I hear the name, all I can think of are the fantastical hats worn on race day and famously portrayed in the movie *My Fair Lady*. When we got to the school, we found the pictures the headmistress had sent were not of the school at all but of the nunnery. The school itself wasn't anything to rave about.

Don was always very keen to know about the curriculum because he wanted the girls to all go to college and not "have to work in 120-degree heat, like your old man." As the school's headmistress pretentiously described their curriculum as including French, poetry, history, literature, arts, needlepoint, ballet, and etiquette, Don wanted to know where the math and science courses were. Tartly, the headmistress made clear, "We teach young ladies to be young ladies."

To which Don replied as he rose to leave, "I don't want a bunch of mindless females running around me!" And he headed for the door. I made a quick apology to the open-mouthed woman and followed him out.

There was another school, St. Hilda's, that we were very interested in. One of the British women I knew had a sister who went there. It was in the middle of England, about 170 miles from London, and the IPC dinner was happening in a couple of days. The schedule was adjusted. We would stay in London to see the sights and then head up to St. Hilda's.

I had actually planned our trip around this big company ball, which meant in addition to all our normal clothes, we were carrying Don's tux and my white chiffon "princess" gown. By this time, I had grown tired of the cast on my arm and couldn't see going to the ball with it. I could move my fingers, so I asked Don to cut it off. He went out and brought a Swiss Army knife with a little saw, and that was that!

Don wanted us all to have the experience of riding on a double-decker bus. One morning he announced, "Today we will all go out on a double-decker bus to the end of the line, and then we will come back by subway." We were thrilled to be up on the top deck seeing all the sights. We ended up far away in the suburbs, got off at the end of the line, and headed down into the underground. Don told the woman at the ticket window where we wanted to go, and she said to take the train with the blue sticker on top. When the next train with a blue sticker arrived, we got on. Instead of going back in a straight line, we went off on an angle. And we went, and we went. We went through areas that were still bombed out from World War II, until we finally arrived at the end of that line. By now it was getting dark, we didn't know where we were, and there was nobody to ask at this station. We climbed the stairs, and as luck would have it, across the street was a police station.

Don left us outside while he went in to ask for directions. Apparently, there was no easy underground route home, so the policeman took us to a bus stop and told us which bus to take. By now, Don had told him all the places we had been, so this wonderful policeman stayed with us until the bus arrived. The policeman made sure we got on it going the right way, explaining to the conductor where we needed to get off, just to be sure this time we would make it back to our hotel. Finally, we arrived in the center of London, everyone hungry and thirsty from our double-decker bus experience. The first thing we did was buy some sausage rolls and drinks, then went up to our rooms, falling exhausted into our beds.

More adventures ensued, including the changing of the guards at Buckingham Palace, the Crown Jewels at the Tower of London, museums, Big Ben, the Houses of Parliament, Westminster Abbey, and Number 10 Downing Street, the home of the prime minister. We wanted the girls to see as much as possible, and for that matter, so did I.

One stop was Madame Tussauds wax museum. As we were going in to see the life-sized, realistic wax figures, there was a bobby standing there. I said, "Oh, look at the policeman, girls, doesn't he look real." The girls thought so too, and when I turned around to follow the group, a man's arm came out and tapped me on the shoulder: "I'm no slab." Well, I just about landed on the ceiling, and the girls found that ever so funny. At least one of the wax figures really *was* real.

Gala day finally arrived.

I told Don, "Now, today you're not taking that car." He was having enough trouble driving on the wrong side of the road, and no way after a couple of drinks was I going to get in that car with him. He agreed we would take a taxi. I took my bath and then set off to a department store that had a beauty parlor. Don took the girls for the day. I spent hours there. I had a facial and a manicure and a massage on my shoulders and my face. I had the salon put on my makeup, do my hair, while the maid back at the hotel pressed our clothes. When I returned, Don had all the girls in bed, and I took over while he got prepared. All I had to do was slip my dress over my head and I was ready.

Oh boy, I'll tell you, that IPC dinner was something! It was a beautiful, beautiful ballroom. All the women were bejeweled in floor-length formal gowns and the men smart in their stud and cuff-linked tuxes. There must have been five wine glasses at each place setting. I looked across the room, and there was a man with an orchid in his button-hole. One of the men at our table saw me staring at him and quizzed me, "You know who that is, don't you, Lorraine?"

"I haven't a clue."

"That's Gulbenkian. His father founded the Iraq Petroleum Company and was called Mr. Five Percent because he owned 5 percent of all the oil pumped out of Iraq. He always wears an orchid in his lapel." That struck me funny. Perhaps it was the wine. They had wonderful food, wine, and a great, great floor show and then dancing well into the night. We didn't get home until the wee hours of the morning, and Don was very glad he had not driven.

The dirty clothes were piling up again. They said there were automatic laundries like in the States, so I set out with my full suitcase while Don took the girls out. After the wash cycle was complete, I placed the clothes in a little cylinder to spin dry. When it stopped, I reached in and complained to the woman in charge, "There is something wrong with this machine because the clothes are not dry." She dropped another coin in, it spun to life, and when it stopped, I reach my hand in and again complained, "They're still not dry."

"That's as dry as they get. This is semiautomatic."

I was horrified. I now had a suitcase full of wet clothes. That was the longest two blocks back to the hotel. I had to keep putting it down, lifting it, then dragging it along. Remember, suitcases didn't have wheels in those days. I had clothes draped everywhere in our two rooms. The maid must have felt sorry for me because she said, "I will take them and iron them for you." By morning, everything was back, dry, ironed, and ready to go. I bless her to this day.

It was now time for us to pack up and check out St. Hilda's. On the day we left, the car was loaded, with some of the luggage tied on the top and the rest protruding out of the boot. Moments into the trip, Don encountered a roundabout near Buckingham Palace. I can't for the life of me remember the name. We were trying to get on a road that would lead us out of London. Not familiar with roundabouts, he became stuck on the inside lane, going round and round. Don tried to move over but just couldn't. The officer on duty saw me with my hands over my eyes and these four little faces in the back of the car. That policeman finally got the idea that here was somebody who didn't know how to drive in London. On our fifth go-around, he blew his whistle. All the traffic stopped. He held the cars while he motioned Don where he wanted us to go. The kind policeman held all that traffic while we got on our way. I don't know, traveling with Father was something.

Somehow, we arrived at St. Hilda's all in one piece. The school and convent were located near Doncaster on the estate of Lord Halifax. It was an eighteenth-century limestone Georgian country house called Hickleton Hall that had been leased in 1947 to the Order of the Holy Paraclete Convent, who ran St. Hilda's Church of England girls' school. Doncaster is not too far from Leeds in southern Yorkshire. We immediately fell in love with the headmistress, Sister Bridget Mary, and knew we could trust her with our girls. The priest, whose name has slipped my mind, was lovely too. Indeed, all the staff we met were simply wonderful. We spent the afternoon there touring the school, dorms, and talking with them about the courses and about our daughters — Barbara, a bright, tall, lanky, blonde ten-year-old who suffered from a lack of coordination that made her feet fly out to the side when she tried to run. And Deedee, a petite, brunette nine-year-old with amazing coordination, who struggled and worked so hard at learning in school. They were quite the opposite.

We discovered during the conversation that with our Atlantic reservations having fallen through and the soon-to-be-upon-us beginning of the school year, we could not take Barbara and Deedee back to the States with us and return in time for the start of the term. We explained our dilemma, and Sister Bridget Mary offered, "Why don't you check them in a few days early. We'll be happy to take care of Barbara and Deedee until school starts." She felt certain they should be there for the first day of class and not arrive late.

There was much to do to get them ready. Don found another house nearby where we could stay, and the woman here too was very nice. We were so lucky we could find people who would take in this huge family. We had been given a list of clothing to purchase. I think there were eight pairs of shoes required for each girl including Wellingtons, plimsolls (a type of athletic shoe with a canvas upper and rubber sole), Sunday shoes, and school shoes. And their Sunday dress looked like it had been designed in 1890! There was a school coat, school hat, and school uniform for during the week. There were underclothes and socks. Personal items and a shoe polishing kit to shine their shoes each week. The list was so long it made for a horrible shopping trip!

We had to go to a larger town nearby to do all the shopping. Their coats, hats (berets), and school uniforms all had to be ordered. We also had to buy each of them an eiderdown (comforter). Not only did we have to buy all those things, every individual item had to be labeled with each girl's name. We brought our huge shop back to the house. Each evening, after the girls went to bed, Don and I sewed on labels. We were sewing them on by hand. Then the woman who was hosting us offered her sewing machine. It was an old hand-crank type. I felt I was faster doing it by hand, but Don stuck with the crank machine because it was more fun for him, I guess. Somehow, we got it all done.

In the meantime, Don had to take a day to go into London to find another way across the Atlantic. When he returned, he had booked passage to New York on a German ship, the *Hanseatic*. It was a one-class ship, where all passengers received the same quality rooms/berths and facilities. He made reservations both ways with three or four weeks in between, so we could go on to California.

It was now time to leave the girls at school. That was the hardest thing I ever did in my entire life. I can still see them standing there with Sister Bridget Mary in the center, an arm around each one's shoulder, and Deedee just mouthing, "Mummy, Mummy," as we drove away.

On the drive back to London, I just plain couldn't talk because I was sitting there with tears streaming down my face. I didn't want Kathy and Pam to think we were doing something terrible leaving their sisters in boarding school as next year Kathy would be joining them and Pam after that. So Don kept up a cheerful conversation with them while I was going "sniffle." I managed to make it back to London without a complete breakdown. The next day, we turned in the car in Southampton and boarded our ship. My only solace was knowing that I would see Barbara and Deedee on our return in about six weeks.

ST. PANCRAS OLD CHURCH, KING'S CROSS, LONDON

I could identify with my mom's appreciation of people's kindnesses. Sometimes things do not go to plan, and it is the chance encounters with thoughtful strangers that get one through. I have many more examples of those occurrences than I could possibly recount and an equal number that I have probably forgotten. Yet I had occasion to reflect on these kindnesses one morning on a two-plus-hour train ride to Leeds, a city just north of where my sisters had been left in boarding school.

The meeting was with ASDA (Wal-Mart's superstore brand in the U.K.) to present a healthy-eating concept for our upcoming animated movie *Monsters vs. Aliens*. This was a mammoth project that had taken a couple of months to put together. So here I was with my innovative program in hand, meeting secured. It was earlier than I would have preferred, requiring me to wake at 5:00 a.m. to make all the connections and be in Leeds by 10:00 a.m.

I don't even remember the wake-up call that morning. The next thing I knew my backup alarm, room service, was knocking at my door. I bolted for the bathroom to get ready lickety-split. I raced out of the hotel, ran-walked up the hill to Green Park underground station, and down the escalators onto the platform. Gasp! The doors had just that instant hissed closed. Not making this train meant I would miss my train to Leeds. The train began to move when suddenly it stopped and the doors reopened. Perhaps the operator saw the horror on my face, or maybe it was because I was the only one on the platform, running flat out to catch the last carriage. Whatever the reason, I waved my thanks when the doors reopened and jumped on board. This is the only time in my hundreds, maybe thousands of underground rides that I have ever seen a train stop after the doors were closed and it had begun moving. What a miracle. It would be tight, but now I had a chance to make that Leeds train.

We pulled into King's Cross underground station, and again I was off and running, down the platform, up the escalator to look at the departure board. Gasp again! My train was off the board with the flap display doing a reset, which meant it was gone. I just couldn't miss that train! My only thought was to run to the platform the Leeds train had left from the last time, which luckily was right behind the departure board. The gate was closed, and the train dispatcher was blowing his whistle. I asked the guard at the gate, "Is this the train to Leeds." He nodded. "Please, sir, I have to catch this train," He waved his hands. I must have looked pretty desperate, because he opened the gate and let me board the last car. "Thank you! Thank you so much." The train immediately lurched and chugged out of the station while I lurched and chugged the three train cars to my seat. I was breathless and amazed. I had two hours and twenty minutes to marvel at what had just occurred, and that caused me to recall some of the other times the kindness of a stranger had helped me to find my way.

When I was sixteen, I went to visit my sister Kathy, who was studying at the University of Tübingen in the south of Germany as part of her college course at Antioch College. In a letter, she had drawn a map of how to find her dorm from the train station. I was standing on a street corner, attempting to get my bearings, when a young woman walked up and asked in English, "Can I help you?" (Did I really look that American?)

"Yes, please. I am looking for my sister, and she gave me this map." The young woman took the map, seemed to know right where to go, and walked me up the hill to the dorm. This was a fifteen-minute walk. Not only that, she inquired of some students where my sister's dorm was, accompanied me upstairs, and made sure I was safe in Kathy's care before she left. I'm sure I was not on her list of things to do that morning, yet she interrupted her plans to help me and then resumed her original course. I've never forgotten.

That same summer, I was trying to get to Málaga to visit another sister, Deedee, who was studying Spanish for her bilingual teaching credential in college. There was a conductor who would not let me on the train. The train from Madrid split in Córdoba with half going to Seville and the other half to Málaga. He directed me farther down the line to another carriage and another conductor. This conductor also would not let me board. Apparently, these cars held the reserved seats. But this was the only unlocked Málaga carriage I could find.

I waited until the conductor was showing a passenger to his seat, and I climbed on board. He saw me and gave chase. Desperate, I grabbed a stranger. "Do you speak English?" He nodded, a bit surprised. My problem tumbled out of my mouth while I clung to him, and the conductor tugged on me. The stranger sorted it out, convincing the conductor to find me a place in the crowded, I-can-barely-breathe, unreserved-seats carriage. As if this kind stranger had not done enough already, when the train got under way, he returned and invited me to his uncrowded reserved section. I traveled in relative comfort for the seven hours it took to get to Málaga. Some young soldiers joined our compartment halfway through the trip. When I arrived, Deedee was there to meet me as I tumbled from the carriage with six young men in tow. I explained to Deedee how they all looked after me during the journey. Deedee thanked them in Spanish for taking care of her "little sister" (I was five inches taller than her at this point). Walking out of the train station, she teased, "And to think I was a bit worried about you!"

I can name dozens more of these times when strangers went out of their way to help me. My mom has many such stories of her own. Princess Diana is quoted as saying, "Carry out a random act of kindness, with no expectation of reward, safe in the knowledge that one day someone might do the same for you." I have been the recipient of much goodwill, and while not always successful, I have made an effort to pay these acts of kindness forward.

I was thinking about all this on my return ride from Leeds. Being so close to my sisters' old boarding school had triggered lots of memories. I was very tired when we pulled into King's Cross and was looking forward to a room service dinner, my pajamas, and turning in early that night. But I also wanted to take a walk, having been sitting for five of the last eight hours. I set off to go exploring. I exited King's Cross onto Euston Road and took a right on Midland Road, passing alongside St. Pancras station. As the road curved, a comely green space came into view. It was raised above street level, and there appeared a church with a placard saying "All Welcome." The steps were set at an angle to the sidewalk as if to sweep all passersby up the stairs into its tranquil garden. It doesn't take much for me to want to enter a churchyard, for as you know by now, I cannot resist a church.

St. Pancras Old Church is one of the most ancient sites of Christian worship in London. Its informational post said that during the civil war — Wait . . . what civil war? All I could think of was the American Civil War and had to laugh. Of course, other countries had civil wars, but it sounded so odd. The English Civil War predates the American Civil War by more than two hundred years! So during the English Civil War in the 1640s, the church was used as a barracks and stable for Cromwell's troops.

In the churchyard, there was a massive old ash encircled by hundreds of overlapping mossy gravestones that the tree roots appeared to be consuming. Again, according to an informational posting, in the mid-1860s, the railway lines were being expanded through part of the graveyard and that required the relocation of many bodies. English novelist Thomas Hardy, of *Far from the Madding Crowd* fame, was working for the firm contracted to handle this delicate job. Hundreds of headstones remained when the work was finished (leads one to ponder what happened to all those bodies), and Hardy arranged the headstones in a circle around an ash that today is called the Hardy tree.

Into the church I went to have a look around. There were some centuries-old wood carvings throughout and hard wooden chairs on which to sit. As I crossed the threshold, I stumbled, catching my shoe on my ever-present briefcase rolling too close behind. This lovely woman put out her hand to steady me, smiled, and exited to my soft "Thank you." Here again, I was made aware of the kindness of a stranger. It had just been a day for it. I sat and thought about my mother.

I learned about the kindness of strangers from my mother for, so many times, it was the kindness of strangers that got us through. My mother's stories about how people helped us during our travels made me open to receiving such support in my own life. She saw the world and its people as basically good and gave that same perspective to us all. That day, as I lit my candle, I thanked her for teaching me to see people as good and kind, for indeed most are.

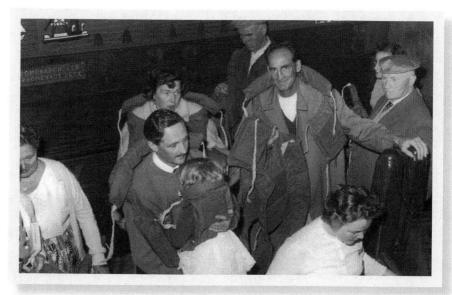

Lifeboat drill before the hurricane
Lorraine and Don

Last photo on the *Hanseatic* before Hurricane Helene hit

17 "I hope we live through this": First leave, part 3

LORRAINE — HOME LEAVE, 1958: THE ATLANTIC

The *Hanseatic* was a good ship, although it was certainly not as big or luxurious as the *Queen Mary* or the *Queen Elizabeth*. I was disappointed and remained angry with our Iraqi travel agent for losing out on the chance to travel aboard those regal ocean liners. The first day and a half on board the *Hanseatic* was wonderful. The first night, we had a good dinner in the dining room, and it was jam-packed. There was a whole table full of nuns that had come from Ireland and were going to the United States. There were a couple of priests too. After dinner, we moved upstairs with the girls to enjoy the evening's entertainment. Kathy and Pam ended up dancing in what was called a "sausage line" — everyone gets in a line with their hands on the waist or shoulders of the person in front and hop and kick their legs to the side in rhythm to the music. The girls thought this was great fun, and we enjoyed a wonderful evening.

The next day, it started to get rough, and by the evening, it *was* rough. We were in the middle of a hurricane. It was Hurricane Helene.* Believe me when I say that the *Hanseatic* bounced. She rode the waves down into the valleys, then climbed back up, only to tilt forward and do it over and over again. Sometimes you would see a foam-topped mountain of seawater coming at you only to have

---

* Hurricane Helene was the most intense tropical cyclone of 1958 — a category 4 hurricane with winds of 150 miles per hour. We were to the north of the worst part, intersecting it when it was classified as a category 1 storm with winds in the seventy-four to ninety-five miles per hour range.

it crash over the ship. No one could go out on deck. The deck chairs broke away from their anchors and were flying all over the place before being washed out to sea. That evening, few people made it to the dining room.

The next morning after breakfast, I was standing by a door, holding on, watching the waves crash about us, and thinking, "I hope we live through this." One of the priests came up and stood there talking with me. Suddenly, a woman rushed up.

"Father, Father, are you going to say mass?"

In his Irish brogue and a twinkle in his eye, he replied, "How can I say mass? I can't get the candles to stand up." His little joke did not calm her. Instead she started to get hysterical, so he turned to me and said, "I'll see you later." He took her down to her room and probably said a prayer or did mass to help her survive her panic.

Our cabin had two bunk beds. That evening, we put the girls in the top bunk to sleep and headed to the bar for a nightcap. The bar was at the front of the ship with glass windows all around to afford beautiful oceanic views . . . on an ordinary cruise. But now one of the windows had been blown out, setting bottles and the bartender flying. He broke his wrist in the mayhem. The window was quickly boarded up, but other windows were cracked and cracking all around us. Some people were there with their pets, mostly dogs, because the ship stewards had to bring them in from the kennels located out in the storm at the top of the ship. A woman who was sitting and chatting with us had heels on. She got up and said, "This isn't improving. I'm going down to put on some flat shoes." She didn't come back, and she didn't come back. Don went down to check on her. We knew what floor she was on, so he asked the steward about her.

"Oh, she is in the sick bay. She fell coming down the stairs, and we think that she's broken her ankle."

Don came back to tell me what had happened. While

we were talking, two little figures came into the bar in their pajamas, Kathy and Pam. Kathy was so indignant! "Daddy, we can't sleep. The storm won't let us. Pammy keeps flying out of that bed, and I have to climb down and catch her so she won't fall." Apparently, Pam would grab ahold of the edge when she was thrown about and would then hang there until Kathy came to lift her down. We knew that was enough. We had better go down to the cabin with them.

When we arrived at the room, I asked, "Okay, which one are you going to take?" Pam slept more restlessly, so Don took Kathy in the top bunk. I took Pam in the bottom bunk, and we slept. The next morning, there was water flowing down the halls. By this time, I was getting a little concerned. The weather wasn't letting up, and we were not making much headway. No one seemed to know what the heck was going on.

On through the next day and the next, the weather raged on. Even the furniture that was chained down broke away. The crew installed ropes along the stairs for the passengers to grab onto so we wouldn't break our necks. But most people stayed in their cabins to ride out the storm. People weren't eating. The only ones in the dining room morning, noon, and night were the Newton family. We always made it. This morning, there was no more hot breakfast. Our waiter explained, "We don't dare turn on the stoves. It is just too bad." They managed some coffee and brought rolls and bread to eat. There was cold cereal for the girls, but that was the best they could do under the circumstances.

Finally, we pulled into New York Harbor. We were seventy-two hours overdue. The captain was honored for bringing the ship through, as well he should have been. When we were waiting for our luggage, we watched the cars being lifted out of the hold. They were wrecks. I'll never forget this little Volkswagen that looked like an accordion when it emerged. People were coming off on crutches and in wheelchairs. There were broken wrists and ankles. People had been sick all over the ship. I was just glad we Newtons were such good sailors.

We had booked our return passage before we left the U.K. I told Don there was "no way in hell" I would get back on that ship to return to England. He went to the shipping office to tell them his wife would not get back on the ship. "Oh, but, sir, we will have it all fixed. All the windows and things repaired before it goes across again."

"I'm sorry, my wife just won't go." He received a refund. He walked across the road to the Holland America Line and secured passage on the *Ryndam* for our European return, after our visit to California. But the funny thing was the *Hanseatic* became the College of the Seven Seas for Chapman University in California several years later. It was still going across the ocean, and it was still bringing people through for many, many years. But I sure was a coward. I would not get back on that ship for all the tea in China.

It was now mid-October, and I thought it would be lovely to see the fall colors by taking a bus to Duluth, Minnesota, to visit my sister. Don wasn't going for this at all. He said, "You go ahead and go. You see your sister in Duluth, and I'll see mine in California."

"Okay. I'll take a bus to Duluth because I want the girls to see the fall colors. Then we'll catch a train to California and meet you there." I must have been crazy. By this time, we had been on the road almost three months. I called my sister Arlene and told her we were coming.

The next morning, we stopped for breakfast before Don put us on the bus. It was a culture shock, believe me, coming from Europe and the Middle East, where we had formal settings for breakfast, to go into a restaurant and someone slaps down a glass of water on a bare table with no silverware and says, "What'll you have?" The girls wanted doughnuts. Oatmeal and milk would have been a better choice, but we let them have doughnuts and milk, and then left to catch our bus.

Here was Kathy, who had been through a hurricane, on all different kinds of rides and things, never once being sick. We were hardly out of New York when she threw up her toenails in the bus restroom. She was not feeling well and missed most of the fall colors I so wanted her to see. It was a long bus ride from New York to Duluth, but we got there all right. We spent about a week visiting. I had to buy the girls jeans with flannel linings because it was much colder in Minnesota. One of the adventures Kathy and Pam enjoyed the most was raking up the leaves and leaping from the porch into the pile.

By the time we got to California, we only had about two weeks there. We saw our friends, exchanging stories over countless cups of coffee. Don even got in a couple of rounds of golf. All too soon it was time to catch the plane to New York to board the *Ryndam* for Southampton.

Our departure was scheduled for November 18. The *Ryndam* was also a one-class ship like the *Hanseatic*. It was a Dutch ship, very nice and so clean. We had a cabin with a toilet and a sink, but you had to make an appointment to take a bath. There was a lady in the bath who would scrub your back. The girls didn't think this was so hot, having a strange lady scrub their backs. She would scrub their backs, hand them to me, and then scrub my back really good. I thought it was quite nice.

It was a calm crossing this time. Uneventful, which we all enjoyed. Don always loved traveling by ship because he didn't have to do anything. All he could do was relax, and he loved that! As soon as we arrived, we grabbed a train into London and another up to Doncaster to see the girls. We spent a couple of days with them, and it was such a joy. But then we had to go through saying good-bye to Barbara and Deedee all over again. That was so hard, because

I knew we wouldn't see them again until July, when they would fly out for the summer. It just tore me apart.

ST. SARKIS, KENSINGTON, LONDON, ENGLAND

I don't know how my mother could call herself a coward. She survived the revolution and then found herself in Hurricane Helene, all the while maintaining her composure. If she was worried about us living through the hurricane, I'm sure she was also worried about leaving my two oldest sisters as orphans. But one would never know she had any concerns. Every day, we got up, dressed, and went to breakfast. Then we read, colored, and played through to the end of an "ordinary" day. Just as we did during the revolution. I felt no fear emanating from either of my parents, resulting in a calm, business-as-usual air about this stormy and turbulent crossing on board the *Hanseatic*.

I find turbulence can come in many forms, and we were experiencing some turbulence at the office. One thing I was taught was loyalty. One never speaks ill of family. If there was a problem, it was handled in the home. In a way, your team at the office was like your family, and our boss was like a parent. Unfortunately, office families can be fraught with office politics. Navigating the waters of office politics has always been tricky for me, so my answer is to stay out of the fray.

There is another interesting parallel between a family and a work environment — the jockeying to be the favorite when you have a reasonable boss and the banding together to help one another when you don't. Most of us had run afoul of our boss at some point, and some of those episodes resulted in dismissals. I have managed a large team, and I have had the unfortunate responsibility of firing staff. I also know from experience that management supports their managers, who need to build the teams they think will do the job best. I believed the company would back our boss. The best I could do was continue to support my colleagues as they had always supported me.

Unfortunately, after having observed the cycle of colleague firings several times, we all realized no one was safe. The pattern became clear, and the warning signs of an approaching storm were apparent. Toward the end of my tenure, I was asked by a colleague, who saw the warning signs, to support her in an action against our boss. I declined, not because I thought her complaint had no merit, but because I felt my loyalty lay with our boss. Our boss had hired me with such faith that I didn't even have to interview for the position, and it was at a time when I was out of work and unsure of my future. The second reason was that California is an at-will employment state, which means, absent an agreement or statutory exception, an employer may terminate an employee for any reason at any time. The alliance with my colleague would be ill-advised. As a California employee, I did not have the legal protections my colleagues had in the U.K. My final reason was my belief that anytime I felt I could not support my boss, it was time for me to quit, not the other way around.

My colleague was disappointed. And to be honest, I was questioning my decision. Was I a coward? Were my reasons simply justifications? Should one be loyal to the boss even to the point of a shipwreck? In this scenario, my colleague's answer was to mutiny, while mine would be to jump ship. Neither one felt right.

Our boss and the licensing group president were in London for a review of the European licensing program. A team dinner was scheduled in Knightsbridge, an upscale area of London, for that evening. After the meal, my colleague lodged her complaint with our president. I walked back to my hotel with a heavy heart.

I did not sleep well that night. When I woke, I wanted some quiet time in a church and knew where I wanted to go. St. Sarkis is an Armenian church built by Calouste Gulbenkian, the same man who founded the Iraq Petroleum Company. He built this church in honor of his parents. I had read about it in my research on Gulbenkian for my book and had wanted to see it for a long time. It was easy to get to, just around the corner from High Street Kensington station, so off I went.

St. Sarkis had a powerful squareness about it and a cool white stone interior. It looked very different from the Romanesque and English Gothic churches I most often found myself in. As I sat there, I reflected. Everything about this situation felt awful. My colleague was also my friend. We had been there for each other through some pretty challenging times. All my mother's teachings about what it means to be a friend came flooding in. And I felt even worse.

There was no win here as I believed the outcome was assured. It would only be a matter of time. I just hoped our friendship would survive. It was going to be a very unpleasant number of months while the tempest ran its course.

I went to the candles and stood for a while. I wasn't feeling very grateful, just sad (and not for the first time). What lesson was there in all this? I wondered. Maybe none. Maybe it was just knowing that if Mom was alive, she would have been there for me. I could go to Mom when I was troubled, and she comforted me. Feeling her love and support, I lit my candle. Thanks, Mom, for being there when I needed you most.

Aboard the *Ryndam*
Don, Pam, Lorraine, Kathy

18 "I wonder how we did it": First leave, part 4

Don made plans for another ship from Southampton to Vigo, Spain. Then we were going to go across Spain into France and take another ship from Marseilles through the Mediterranean to Beirut with the final stop being Kirkuk, home. On the crossing to Vigo, we befriended another lady like Miss Alice, who had helped us so much in Austria. She had been studying English in England and was returning to teach English in Spain. As we were chatting, she said she was going across Spain by train. Don thought, "Oh, that sounds like fun." I had read in an article that you should never go across Spain by train and certainly not second class. Well, we traveled with our new friend to Madrid, and of course, we ended up in second class! There was no food, so at each stop, Don and the woman would leap off and get sandwiches and bottles of wine. There was no bottled water, and they never seemed to find any soda pop. With only wine to drink, the girls had a happy trip!

We all stayed together in Madrid. One day, we went to a flea market with our traveling companion, and the girls saw two cute parakeets, a blue-and-white one and a green one, in a tiny wooden cage. Of course, Don bought his little girls those parakeets. We added the parakeets to the two little American flags we purchased in New York, along with two Hula-Hoops and all the luggage we were hauling back to

Kirkuk. The woman said parakeets weren't allowed on trains and planes, but that is how we were traveling. We placed them under our seats, hoping no one would find them. And no one did. I warned Kathy at the start, "If anybody takes those parakeets away, you can't cry because we're not supposed to be taking them across borders." Kathy agreed she wouldn't cry, although she was absolutely certain she could sneak those birds home to Kirkuk.

We left our wonderful Spanish friend in Madrid while we continued to Barcelona. As we headed into the city, the train stopped. Don said, "Oh, we're here."

I disagreed, "No, this isn't a big enough station."

"Oh, yes, it is," and he herded us all off the train. When Don tried to tell the porter to take our luggage off, the porter simply slammed the baggage compartment closed, the train started up and took off. There we stood on this platform with no luggage. Don went into the station and found somebody who spoke enough English to understand him. Back he came to quickly corral us into the nearest cab. "Follow that train. Fast, please," he urged the cab driver, "Our luggage is on it." Apparently, we had alighted at a station on the outskirts of the city. When we arrived at the main train station, the train was already there. Don raced to get our luggage. I think I may have already mentioned that traveling with Father was something.

We made Barcelona our base for exploring the surrounding sights. We went to Montserrat, home to the Black Madonna sculpture. There were two legends that I had heard about her. The first was that when the Benedictine monks were building their abbey, the statue became too heavy to move, and they had to build around it. The other was that she was carved in the early days of Christianity in Jerusalem, but archaeologists dispute that. Either way, the Black Madonna, considered a patron of Spain, was revered and something important to see. Also, this is the home of the renowned Montserrat Boys Choir. The boys sounded, to me, as wonderful as the Vienna Boys Choir. Their voices were just radiant. Outside the monastery was a tram that went up the sheer rock of the mountain at Montserrat. Not me! My knees turned to water just at the mere sight of it. Don took the girls, and I waited for them.

We were on a tour when we came upon a whole group of cardinals just returned from Rome. One of the cardinals noticed the girls and stopped in greeting. I told Kathy and Pam, "What you do is go up to him, you bow down, and you kiss the ring on his hand." Pam wouldn't but Kathy did. The cardinal gave her a little golden medal which she treasured. Don put it on a bracelet he bought for her. About two days later, we were going down the street, and all of a sudden Kathy stopped and started to cry. She didn't have the medal on her bracelet. We retraced our steps, and we searched and we searched, and we couldn't find it. I saw one that looked similar in a store and sneaked in and bought it. Later I told her we found hers. She knew darn well it wasn't hers and wouldn't have anything to do with it. You couldn't fool that kid for nothing.

While on a bus in Spain, we met another interesting woman, an older American. She was traveling by herself. We got along great, so before we went our separate ways, we exchanged addresses. I extended an invitation, offhandedly, as I had done with others we met on our travels: "If you ever get to Kirkuk, Iraq, come and see us." Imagine my surprise when more than a year later, we got a letter saying she was coming for a visit. We couldn't even remember who she was!

One of the things on my to-do list in Spain was to see a bullfight. Sadly, it was the wrong time of the year for bullfights and not to be.

When we were in Toledo, Spain, we visited a famous factory where they make beautiful inlaid swords. I acquired an intricate miniature set of swords and also a lovely gold inlaid bracelet. While researching our trip, I learned that Toledo had two signature dishes — a suckling pig and a special soup with an egg in the center of each bowl. Naturally, we ordered each one. None of us were thrilled with the soup. When the pig arrived, it was whole, skinned, with its head on, and a red apple in its mouth. The girls said, "Look at the cute little piggy." It was so fatty we couldn't eat much of it. At least I got to try it.

Dinner in Spain is served very late by American standards. They don't start until 10:00 p.m., but that was too late for Kathy and Pam. We started feeding them their main meal at noon and then convinced the hotel to bring to our room a cheese omelet, glass of milk, and a scoop of ice cream for each girl at 7:00 p.m. We'd put them to bed and then go downstairs to have our dinner. There was so much olive oil on everything, Don finally talked to the chef and ordered us grilled fish with a salad every night instead. Don asked him not to put anything on it — no dressing, no lemon juice, just plain. And it was good. That's just kind of late for us to eat.

And we still had those darned birds. One night after we left, the girls let them out of the cage and then fell sound asleep. Don had put some socks to soak in the sink. When we returned, we discovered one had fallen into the soapy water, and just his little beak was showing. We fished him out, dried him off, and laid him on the radiator. You know, the darn thing recovered. It was never sick or anything.

We left Spain and flew to Marseilles, France, to catch our boat for our zigzag tour of the Mediterranean. We checked into a hotel for three days, only to find out there was no dining room — they had no kitchen. The next morning, Don woke up, and he was so sick. He thought it was a reoccurrence of the jaundice, and I thought he had malaria. He was sweating and burning up with fever. I called the chambermaid to change his sheets about four times a day.

At first, he didn't want anything to eat, and I'd go out and get him some orange juice. There was a restaurant down the street where the girls and I ate. I talked to the owner, explaining that my husband was ill and I wanted to take him some food. Don wanted a steak and potatoes, so I got it for him, and a roll. The man covered the tray, and I took it back up to the room. Don couldn't eat much of it, but he tried because he was determined to get on that ship. He worried, "They won't let me on the ship if I'm sick. And I know once I get on the water, I'll be all right."

Those were the least pleasant few days of our whole trip, of course. How he made it out of bed and got dressed and into and out of the cab and onto that ship I will never know. It was sheer determination. Once on the ship, he went to bed. Just one day on the water and he was feeling so much better. He would sit up on deck, breathing in the sea air and napping.

We were supposed to cruise from Marseilles to visit the island of Cyprus. Well, there was trouble on the island of Cyprus, so they wouldn't let us off the ship. Cyprus, under British rule at that time, was experiencing a flare-up by the Cypriot population in an ongoing push for independence. While sitting offshore, some men from the British army boarded the ship. They communicated with their base via ship-to-shore radio, and they let Kathy and Pam talk ship-to-shore too. The girls thought that was just grand.

We went on to Alexandria, Egypt. We didn't see the pyramids because we weren't in Cairo, but we saw Alexandria and the fascinating antiquities at the museum. We hired a guide and a car and drove around the city. As we were driving down a street, I saw a cart with sweet potatoes cooking. I had never seen them over in the Middle East. Fresh ones. Immediately, I called for the man we had hired, the guide, to "Stop the car."

"What for?"

"I want you to go buy me two of those." He looked at me like I was crazy. No Americans buy off street vendors. I figured they were in their skins, so how dangerous could it be? Of course, there was no butter and no salt. He brought them back with a napkin or something for us to eat it with, and we broke them apart. They tasted absolutely wonderful, even with nothing on them. We enjoyed them so much that when he dropped us off exploring someplace, he went back to that vendor and bought us a big grocery sack as a gift. I took the sack on board the ship with me along with a beautiful brass tray 28½ inches round I fell in love with and Don bought for me. We set sail once again.

From there we went to Greece. We docked in Piraeus to spend the day in Athens, arriving by bus from the ship. While we saw the ruins, Don sneaked away. It was Kathy's eighth birthday, December 17, and he wanted to get her a gift. He bought her a little wristwatch. Then when the tour group was in downtown Athens, I snuck away. When I saw caps just like the sailors wore on the ship in a window, I bought one for her. Then I saw a shop with some sweets in it. I got four little net things tied with candied almonds on the inside and a couple of other small things that could function like favors. There were two little Arab girls on the ship, and I thought we'd give Kathy a small birthday party.

I gave the ship's cook some yams to make for the celebration, and I told him how to bake them. He cooked them until there was hardly anything left inside but redeemed himself with the delightful cake he created. I had these sweets and this cap and her watch to add to the festivities. Kathy loved the watch, but she loved that cap more. She was quite the take-charge little tomgirl. When the captain saw Kathy's hat, he laughed. He told me I had purchased a Greek schoolboy's cap for my little girl. While the candies, I was informed, were a traditional sweet at Greek weddings, not for a child's birthday party. Oh well. She didn't know the difference, and they served their purpose.

The four little girls were the only children on board the ship for the whole of the cruise. In fact, I can't think of another woman on the ship other than the mother of these two girls and me. There were no women staff. This was a Greek ship. There were cabin boys, and all the other help was male. There was no playroom with an attendant either like we had enjoyed crossing the Atlantic, so the other mother and I would stay up on deck and watch the girls play, making sure they didn't fall overboard or something. With just the two of us talking all day, we became quite friendly.

She had an interesting story to tell. Her husband was a Syrian diplomat based in England who had been recalled. She had her PhD in literature and was a Palestinian. She told me about her father, who once owned a whole block of the main street in downtown Jerusalem. It had been taken away from him, and he was not paid for it, which she resented very much. She also told me that anybody who wasn't Jewish carried a card. If they were Palestinian or any other Arab, they would have to carry a card indicating they were second-class citizens. They left their son in boarding school in England; only their young daughters were returning with them. They planned to get off the boat in Beirut but were choosing not to go back to Syria. There had been a change in the government, and she was afraid her husband would end up in prison or be killed. It seemed no one was really safe from the evolving turmoil of Middle Eastern politics.

One day, as we were standing watching the girls play and looking out at the beautiful turquoise water of the Mediterranean, she turned to me out of the blue and asked, "Why did you drop the atomic bomb?"

Why did I? Well, I said, "I personally didn't drop it, but it saved a lot of lives, and it was my government. My government, right or wrong, is my government." With that, the woman moved on to a more agreeable subject.

Hoops, birds, and a big brass tray. When we got off the ship in Beirut, we still had those damn birds. Every time we went through customs or we had to get on or off planes, trains, and boats, here was this little cage. Hot or cold, Kathy would put on her red coat, hide them underneath, and double over like she had a stomachache. Often it worked to our advantage, as they rushed us through customs. Kathy managed to bring the parakeets all the way to Kirkuk, and was she pleased. Of course, Don went out and got a nice big cage for them once we were home.

We had taken some schoolbooks with us on the trip to keep Kathy from getting behind in her studies. We didn't worry too much because she was rather a clever little girl, but we made sure that she kept up with her reading and sums while we were on our leave. Not consistently, because she didn't really need that, plus we felt that she was getting more out of the trip than anything. Pam too. She was scheduled to start kindergarten. Missing a couple of months there did not really concern us. We knew she could catch up with her classmates.

We were walking toward a taxi in Beirut when Don saw some children playing with Hula-Hoops, and then he noticed two little ragged children without any. He walked over to give them the Hula-Hoops, saying to me, "Damn, I'm tired of hauling them." We were within one plane ride from home, having carted them all the way back from America, and he gives them away. "Look. They're all around here, so they're available in the Middle East. We'll buy the girls another set when we get to Kirkuk." The taxi delivered us to the company guest house. We spent the night there before we caught the company plane home. As it would turn out, we never did find any Hula-Hoops in Kirkuk.

I had given the key to the locked bedroom where our personal things were stored to a friend of mine. Hassan knew what day we were due home. My friend cleared it with the company so Hassan could get in the house a couple of days before us. The marvel that was Hassan arranged everything for our return. At this point, we had been on the road for four and a half months. It was Christmastime; we were finally back. As I reflect now on this very extensive trip, I wonder how we did it.

SAN JERÓNIMO EL REAL, MADRID, SPAIN

There are just so many things that can happen on the road. I visited Spain less often as it was a smaller business territory for us, usually spending only a day and a night. Once when I landed in Madrid, I had a car ordered to take me directly to a meeting at Carrefour Spain, one of the top ten retailers in the world. The office was between the airport and the city. The Westin Palace hotel had arranged my transportation so after dropping me at the meeting the driver could deliver my luggage. My agent would drop me off later at the hotel. We set off from the airport on our fifteen-minute drive. Twenty minutes into the trip, nothing was looking familiar. I'd been there several times before, and I knew landmarks I should have been seeing. I inquired if there was a problem, but my driver said we would be there soon. Hmmm . . . I called my agent. "Julian, will you please speak with my driver? I think he is lost. I'm afraid I'll be late." After several calls, I arrived — very late indeed. Thank goodness the Spanish are so gracious.

I could only imagine that the driver told his superiors of our late arrival to my meeting because when I checked in to the hotel that night, I had been upgraded to the most breathtakingly beautiful palatial suite in which I have ever been privileged to lodge. I entered via a long hallway, passing a guest toilet before arriving in a splendid living room. To the right were double doors that led into the sleeping quarters. I first found two changing areas with separate bathrooms and closets that put my little ones at home to shame. Through another set of double doors, I finally arrived at the king-size bedroom. Brocades and gold leaf trim adorned the rooms. Intricate molding and wainscoting completed the grand decor. Why was I always alone when such dazzling treats came my way? I was so sad to check out the next morning. After a day of meetings, I would be on my way to Paris.

The tradition of eating late that my mom first encountered so many years ago in Spain continues to this day. It was challenging for our agents because there were few places, except my hotel, where we could dine as early as I preferred. Over time, late lunches became our chosen meal to share. I could see why my parents were challenged to find a clever way to feed Kathy and me in some of the southern European cities. Their day didn't end with our bedtime. Mom and Dad wanted to go out and experience the night life! She was determined to make the most of every moment.

Another time, I decided to fly into Madrid a day early and go to the Prado Museum. It was Sunday, and since Spain is primarily a Catholic country, the museum was closed. I bought a ticket on the Hop-on, Hop-off bus around the city just to see other national sites — also closed. I never did get to the Prado.

On another journey, I went to Retiro Park. I kind of stumbled on it one summer evening when I was out for a walk. There was an open-air rotunda hosting an impromptu gathering of musicians and drummers. Such a joy just to stand and listen. I looked around and saw the pond in the park, and I suddenly realized my parents, Kathy, and I had been there together oh so long ago. I searched my memory banks for some glimmer of a recollection. Alas, none came as I heard my mother's words recounting the visit as if for the first time. Another of those serendipitous moments that opened in front of me.

The wonders even extended to a light dusting of snow during a winter trip. Julian and I watched it fall while in a Toys "R" Us meeting, both of us dressed completely unprepared for such weather. There were little joys like that happening all the time — wonderful, unexpected moments in the middle of all the business hustle and bustle.

The curiosity Mom exhibited and the delights she expressed throughout all her stories showed me how much she loved this time in her life. Looking back, she wondered how she managed a four-and-a-half-month holiday, and I often thought the same of some of my travel. She knew at some point this time would end, and so did I. But there was often wonderful kismet in the unexpected. If the Prado had not been closed, I might not have discovered San Jeróni-mo el Real church across the street.

I stood in front of the candles, thinking about various anecdotes from our family visit to Spain. Not everything was fun in the moment, but so many are funny in the retelling. Like Dad pulling us off the train early in Barcelona and our luggage proceeding on without us. The ensuing "chase that train" taxi ride played out in my mind like one of those old silent movies. My mother clenching the seat in front, openmouthed in horror. My father up front frantically urging the driver to go faster. And my sisters and me (for in my imagination the four of us were always together) flailing our arms in excited delight. I even heard the big chase scene piano music in my head. I lit my candle. I had so much to thank my mom for, but this day, it was going to be for all her memories, so vividly recalled, that allow us to retell them as if we remember these events for ourselves. With Mom as my role model, I was grateful to have learned about the art of storytelling and hope one day to achieve her level of mastery.

Kathy on her horse, Sultan, and stableman

19 "Little donkeys have big ears"

PC had a virtual monopoly on oil exploration and production in Iraq. With the revolution, the company had gone from interacting with a pro-Western government, a monarchy enthroned by the British, to a government founded on Arab nationalism. The Iraqi people felt more and more like they were being exploited by the West. Yet Iraq still needed the expertise the company provided to keep the oil flowing and the government coffers full. Even with some return to normalcy, my parents could feel the winds of change coming, shifting beneath them like the sands of the desert.

LORRAINE — KIRKUK, 1958/1959

The house seemed so empty with only two children in it. I had this unique experience of having one, two, three, four children and then four, three, two, one. And let me tell you, in my opinion, two or four is better than one or three.

We left so quickly after the revolution that in the four and a half months we were gone, there were quite a few changes. Many privileges we had enjoyed before the overthrow of the monarchy could no longer happen or happened infrequently. For instance, we used to be able to hop a company plane to Beirut for the day to have our hair done. I could still make arrangements to go to Beirut to receive some services, only now I'd have to stay overnight. Travel wasn't as free and easy. You had to carry your passport with you. As necessity would have it, I had the girls taken off mine when we got to London, each one of us now had a passport of our own.

There was a different attitude being displayed by many of the Iraqi people, a burgeoning sense of ownership. This new confidence is revealed in a story told by Peggy Nees.

After the revolution, the local people took quite a different attitude to us. They came out to Camp 8 and picnicked in our front yard. They'd just walk in and have a picnic in our garden. One didn't like to go out and say, "Oh, you can't be here. This is my property."

Because they would argue back, "No, this is our property now since the revolution." They would knock on the door and ask for water. They weren't nasty, but it was a funny situation really. I think our houseboy, George, and the other servants thought that soon they would be taking over the houses and they'd be the bosses. But, however, it eventually all settled down, and life went back more-or-less to normal.

The first trip into Kirkuk town after we got back from our leave was really something. I couldn't get any of the women to go with me — they were still afraid of driving into town. With my friends refusing, I decided to venture forth on my own. When I entered the department store, the owner greeted me like a long-lost friend. I guess we had been gone so long they thought we had quit and left. Never! I wanted this adventure to go for as long as possible.

Then I went to the grocery store I liked in town, and oh, was the proprietor ever delighted to see me. I asked him, "I'm going down to the souk, all right?"

"No problem. No problem anymore." Then he questioned, "No Englishi come here. Why Englishi no come?"

"I don't know. I guess they're afraid. I'm not afraid." I went into the souk and got my usual basket boy to carry my purchases. After dropping me off at one end, the car would drive and park at the other end of the souk. He'd wait for me while I walked through and did my shopping. Boy, did I get a welcome from everybody I traded with, and particularly my meat man with his carcasses hanging up, his big knife at his waist, and his Ghazi cigarettes. I always smoked one with him before we would tend to our business. They were so delighted to see me back. It made me feel good. I always thought those merchants were so friendly and so nice. Of course, people are how you treat them too. They knew I was shopping for my family, that I had children. I never felt they ever took advantage of me for anything I bought. It sure beat shopping at Spinneys, the expensive company store.

We were still placed under house arrest at various times but not as often. And there was another thing called curfew. When there was a curfew, we had no cinema. We couldn't go to the club. We had to stay in our house, which put a big crimp on our social life. How do you plan a party if you don't know when you're going to be put on a curfew or under house arrest? We no longer felt as safe getting a car with a couple of women in it and driving to Baghdad for a few days. Just lots of little changes.

There were army soldiers stationed throughout camp. When school resumed after the Christmas holidays, Kathy and Pam would walk up the hill to wait for the school bus. The ever-present soldiers, with their rifles slung over their shoulders, were standing guard.

When the girls returned to school, Kathy's teacher said we should have left Kathy in England. Don said she was too young. The teacher said she's too smart for school here. To which Don objected, "Then you challenge her. That's what you're being paid for." Of course, Kathy couldn't wait to go to boarding school. She wanted to go to school in England like her sisters. Next year she would get her chance.

My girls were always so healthy, but when Barbara and DeeDee went off to boarding school and we just had Kathy and Pam at home, they went through a period of illness. One week they'd be sick; the next week, they'd be getting over it; the next week, back sick again, then getting over it, then well. The company had doctors — an Englishman and an Irishman, a couple of Iraqi doctors, and they had a hospital, the K-1 hospital. We took them to the English doctor. He said that they needed their tonsils out, but he wouldn't do the surgery. He recommended a very fine Indian doctor in town. His name was Dr. Gupta, and he would be given full use of the company's hospital facilities. The staff would cooperate with him, but it would be Dr. Gupta that would have to do the surgery.

Don and I took the two girls into Kirkuk town to see Dr. Gupta. His office was up a stairway, and there was a high examining table in the corner that looked like a steel bed. Sitting behind a desk was this enormous Indian man with a fez — one of those hats that looks like a Shriner — with a tassel. There was a younger Indian man, slim, standing off to the side behind him. We talked to Dr. Gupta and found out that he would charge twenty dinars apiece to take out their tonsils, a little over one hundred U.S. dollars for both the girls. He insisted the girls had to have shots and pills because a big fear over there was infections. Of course, we said, "Fine."

Kathy was quietly sitting and watching and listening to all this when, all of a sudden, she got up and she goes over to this big doctor. She put her little arm around his shoulder. She couldn't reach much further than the center of his back, but she patted him on the shoulder and asked, "Dr. Gupta, just tell me, how are you going to do this operation?"

"I'll tell you, Kathleen, I'm just going to put you to sleep, and I'm going to reach right down your throat, and I'm going to grab those bad old tonsils and get them out of there." I could see her eyes opening wider and wider as he talked. "You won't feel a thing."

Her eyes narrowed. "Dr. Gupta, I may sleep soundly, but I know I wouldn't sleep through that." Then she proposed, "I'll tell you what to do. You take my sister in first and I'll watch. Afterwards, I'll let you know if I want you to do it to me."

By this time, his assistant was doubled over the table in back, he was trying so hard not to laugh. Dr. Gupta's stomach was just going up and down with silent giggles. We told Kathy not to worry. Everything's going to be fine. But before we left, she thought of something else: "Oh, and another thing. I know my teacher at school would love to have these for the science shelf. Would you save them for me in a jar?" He assured her that he would (but he didn't). We made the arrangements for when these tonsils were going to be taken out, shots and everything, and left to prepare.

There was a Little Golden Book we brought with us about a trip to the hospital that I read to them to allay their fears. I had to take them into the hospital the night before this operation was to be performed. I wanted to stay, but the sisters (nurses) wouldn't let me. I told them, "You know, they'll be frightened, and if you'd just let me stay, everything will be all right." No, no. They would call me to come the next afternoon. I worried all night about these little girls in their big, cold hospital beds, but at least the two of them were together.

The next day at noon, I got a call from the head nurse at the hospital asking me to come down and to come right away. I said, "The men are coming home for lunch. I'll come as soon as I can get transportation. What room are the girls in?"

She said tersely, "Just follow the screams."

I thought, "Oh dear." Immediately, I called transportation and said I needed a car, and I needed a driver, and I needed them now. So they got me one. I told Hassan to tell the Sahb (Don) if I wasn't back when he got home from work, that I was at the hospital and for him to come down there.

It was about a twenty-minute drive down to this hospital. The building was one story, T-shaped. When I passed through the front door, there was a long hallway that stretched for what seemed like two blocks, and I could hear one of my daughters screaming. I started running down the hall, and when I got to the end, I turned left towards the screams. I found the room, pushed open the door, and I almost died. There was an Iraqi nurse and an orderly standing back, Pam's lying in bed not saying a word, and Kathy's on the bed straddling her.

Kathy, in all her tomboyishness, loved wearing her dad's old khaki oil field clothes, so I let her bring an outfit to the hospital. I had cut the legs down to fit her. She would put on the pants held tight with one of his big belts, shirt on top. When she did, she transformed into a cowboy or an Indian or just about anything she imagined in that active mind of hers.

As I entered the room, Kathy was standing on the bed with that belt buckle on the outside, swinging it round and round. She was yelling at the top of her lungs, "Don't touch my sister, don't come near me, don't you touch my sister, don't you come near me!"

"Kathleen! What are you doing?"

"Mummy, you didn't tell me it was going to hurt." As soon as she said that, she collapsed on the bed, and boy, did she throw up blood all over. Oh, dear God, I felt so sorry for her.

Of course, Pam in the meantime grabs me and starts to cry. I didn't want her to cry. I got Kathy cleaned up and quieted down and gave Pam a few hugs. By that time, the head nurse had arrived and huffed at me, "Well, thank goodness you're here!"

I turned to her and accused, "I told you I should stay, that they'd be scared, and that all they are is frightened to death to be here." I insisted she bring in another bed. "I will be staying here until my daughters go home." I think we were in there for two or three more days, I can't recall exactly. When

Don came down after work, I sent him back to the house to get my robe, slippers, and nightgown. I just moved in and read them stories. They were no problem whatsoever after that. It was just frightening for them, that's all it was. But you couldn't tell that head nurse that for nothing. She thought we Americans coddled our children. I knew differently.

Peggy commented once about some of the times Kathy and Pam were over at her house playing with her boys: "I always remember Kathy as being rather bossy. She used to organize all the little functions we had at our little tea parties and play times." Kathy did have a tendency to take charge but was never a smart aleck or sassy.

Ava told another story about when Kathy was little and Ava was visiting at bath time.

> I was there one day when Lorraine was givin' all the girls a bath. Kathy had a wishbone and had wished for somethin'. Lorraine was washin' her hair, and I was standin' watching Kathy. I said to Kathy, "Now, dear, what did you wish for?"
>
> "No. I can't tell you, because if I tell you, my wish will not come true."
>
> Lorraine jokes, "Why, Kathy? Is it such a secret? Surely you didn't wish for a million dollars."
>
> And Kathy starts screamin', "How did you guess?! How did you guess?!"
>
> She was only six or seven years old, and she had wished for a million dollars.

Kathy adored Ava's husband, Bobby, and could barely be parted from him when we visited. Ava loved to tell about a time Kathy and Bobby were together.

> The Newton girls had great fun on curry day, except Kathy, because she would just stay sittin' on Bob-

by's knee. She thought he was the most wonderful thing on earth. She loved him to pieces. Once when she was stayin' with us, she wanted to go to bed with Bobby. I said, "You can't go to bed with men, dear."

She replied, "Why not? If I love him enough, I'll go to bed with him."

When you work in a company situation, it's like a small town. You don't want to say anything in front of your children that you wouldn't want them to get up on a stage and announce to everybody. I tried to explain to the girls that if I had guests for tea when they came home from school, they were to politely greet my guests. Then they were to go in their bedrooms, change their clothes, and go out and play with their friends. "When you have your guests, Mommy doesn't come in and play with you and your friends, so you should not stay when I have my friends." I thought I explained it very well.

One day, one of my guests was Toni Shahabonli, an American married to an Iraqi. We were sitting and talking over tea in the living room when the girls came home. Kathy was horse crazy and liked Mrs. Shahabonli because Toni had told her all about having racehorses in Baghdad. Kathy came in with her sisters to say hello. Her sisters excused themselves to go down the hall to their bedrooms. Not Kathy. She sat down on the divan. I said, "Kathleen, go join your sisters."

"No."

"Kathleen, Mommy has guests. Will you please go join your sisters?"

"I don't want to."

A little more forcefully now: "Kathy, I have company and you are not welcome in here."

"Why?"

"Because we have a saying in my country that 'little donkeys have big ears.'"

"But, Mummy, this little donkey doesn't go around telling all the other little donkeys everything she hears."

Well, with that, she took a look at my face and knew she had gone too far. Down the hall she went with me after her. I paddled her, told her to change her clothes, and go outside. I went back to the living room, and my ladies were laughing their heads off. Toni said, "If that kid's smart enough to come up with that, she's smart enough to stay here."

"Oh, no, she isn't."

I couldn't let her get away with that just because she was clever.

IMPERIAL CATHEDRAL BASILICA OF THE ASSUMPTION AND ST. STEPHEN, SPEYER, GERMANY

DreamWorks' in-country licensing agent for Germany, Joachim, and I were in Düsseldorf meeting with a German retailer called Metro. It was early Friday afternoon when we finished. I asked Joachim to drop me at the train station. I wasn't due in Paris until Monday and planned to spend the weekend with Bryan and Susanne Irvine and their girls as I had done numerous times before. The train to Mannheim took only three hours, plus a twenty-minute drive to Heidelberg. Susanne was going to meet me at the station on arrival. If I was lucky, I would make it for dinner.

I love to ride on trains. I can contemplate the great questions of life. Or more often, simply relax without a thought in my mind except the enjoyment of the passing countryside. The first time I observed a solar field in Germany, I was so surprised. It was the middle of winter with snow all around. There, next to the rail lines was a field — not of crops or orchards or the delightful community gardens with their individual plots and little huts but of solar panels. I asked Bryan about this, and he told me that Germans are paid to put solar panels on their roofs. Farmers are paid to "farm" energy via wind turbines, acres of solar panels, and biofuels. Even the fields of yellow-flowered "weeds," I was told, were a part of the plan. The plants are rapeseed, important in biofuel production. As Americans, Bryan and I discussed how Germany was leading the world in this regard, not the good ol' U.S. of A. What is more amazing is that on average Germany gets only 152 sunny days a year, much the same as rainy Seattle. We have an average of 284 sunny days in California. What's our excuse?

Even though I'd ask Susanne not to fuss, she always planned something special that we did as a family. For this visit, she'd come up with a trip to Imperial Cathedral Basilica of the Assumption and St. Stephen, or more simply known as Speyer Cathedral. They wanted me to see the magnificent crypts where the tombs of eight Holy Roman emperors and many German kings are found.

This was breathtaking. Besides the sheer scale of the cathedral, I was awed by the soaring columns of creamy yellow and soft copper-colored sandstone. These columns continued in the crypts below, where I could examine the intricate structure of their alternating sandstone bands. The work involved in cutting the myriad bands of stone in the eleventh century made a lasting impression that comes to mind when I think of Speyer Cathedral. I could see why it is considered one of the most important Romanesque churches in Europe.

As we toured the grounds, Bryan and Susanne's daughters together with a friend were busy being playful sisters. It reminded me of my sisters, and I often thought of Kathy when I was in Germany. She studied biology at the University of Tübingen and worked at the Max Planck Institute in Tübingen during her college years. Mom always said she was the most interesting child to raise. We already know what she thought of me!

As sisters go, we are really close. I think Mom had a lot to do with that. I believe she set the standard early that fighting with your sister was not an option. Barbara and Deedee were very little when they went through a period of aggression and would hit each other. Mom had enough one day and decided to put a stop to it once and for all. Please remember, they were only a year apart, young — two and three years old — and supervised. Under such conditions, the likelihood of any lasting damage was virtually nil.

"Since you two want to fight, we are going to make this fair," Mom explained. "Each of you will take turns hitting the other." She stood them face-to-face and limited the hits to the upper arm. "Okay, Deedee, you hit Barbara." Whack. "Now, Barbara, you hit Deedee." Whack. This went on for a little while, and then they began complaining their arm hurt and they didn't want to hit each other anymore. "Oh, no, since you want to fight, you are going to fight." And the rounds continued.

Pretty soon they were both crying. "I don't want to hit my sister." "I don't want to hit my sister."

"Then remember that the next time you are fighting," Mom admonished. "There'll be no hitting in this house!" Because she set the standard with the two oldest, it transferred down to Kathy and me. I can never remember an occasion of any of us hitting each other. We argued occasionally, but honestly, even those times were rare. As the youngest, they also protected me as Kathy did in the hospital when we were having our tonsils removed. My sisters were my playmates and, to this day, are my best friends. Indeed, I cannot imagine life without them.

I walked over to light a candle. Family relationships are complicated, with interesting dynamics. We were no different. But the one thing Mom taught us was to be a family, to be there for each other — always. We have endured long periods of separation, but we have never been separated in our hearts. Lighting this candle, I thanked Mom for my sisters. "You did a good job, Mom, encouraging us to be close. Of all your considerable gifts, I believe my sisters to be the greatest gift of all."

Deedee and Don
Dancing at the club

20 "Life was great in the summer"

LORRAINE — KIRKUK, 1959

Our family felt cut in half with Barbara and Deedee gone. We longed for that first holiday at the end of July when the girls would come home. The weeks seemed to drag by. Mail call was really something. I so looked forward to the arrival of their letters, as sparse as they were. Every Sunday, the girls were required to write an aerogram, a folding sheet of prestamped lightweight paper in which the letter and envelope are one. Every letter started with, "Dear Mummy and Daddy. How are you? I am fine," followed by "We did so-and-so," written as briefly as possible. These letters did not give us much information, but they were the lifeline to our children.

One day, a letter arrived from Deedee. She had gone to spend a long weekend with her schoolmate Jennifer and Jennifer's family. I was looking forward to hearing news of the fun they had over the holiday. "Dear Mummy and Daddy. How are you? I am fine. I was staying at Jennifer's and her mummy took me to hospital and they cut off half my thumb. I have a sling on. Goodbye." Well, I got that letter and I went hysterical. You couldn't place calls out of the Middle East, otherwise we would have called the girls' boarding school every week and talked to all of them. But it wasn't possible. Nonetheless, I tried then.

I had to do something. I couldn't get through. Naturally, I sat down and wrote Sister Bridget Mary a letter starting, "Dear Sister Bridget Mary. How come you didn't let us know that Deedee had half her thumb cut off?" et cetera et cetera. An agonizing month later, I received her reply, "She had a hangnail removed."

It was very hard to wait but also very hard to write back, because how do you write different letters saying the same thing to two different girls? Which at some point would be four different girls. It was very difficult for me. I found that we lived for that first summer, when we could listen to all their stories and see their faces and hear their happy voices playing together, a family once again.

As the only Americans with children in a British boarding school, our summer holidays mirrored those of our British friends. Together we planned elaborate things for our youngsters. Everybody tried to outdo each other with different types of parties. I remember one party Barbara went to that was a pajama party. They took part in a crazy-hat costume party. Naturally, Kathy wore the parakeets in the little wooden cage on her head, Barbara created a clothesline hat with doll clothes hanging out to dry, and Deedee made a safari hat into a bug protector with netting to the floor and flies glued to the net all around. I devised a Western-style barbecue party. Other people had tea parties and different things for the children. And we spent hours at the pool swimming each afternoon. Life was great in the summer. You'd see every parent in the place beaming all over.

The summer holidays were only six weeks long, and they just flew by. We had acquired a little record player. I don't remember where or how. And with it, several records. One song in particular proved to be a favorite with Deedee. It was a 45 rpm (vinyl) record called "Tell Me We'll Meet Again" performed by glamorous British cabaret singer Lita Roza. Lita crooned about hearts being pulled apart and crying while waiting for you (me) until the day she died. It went on to talk of places where we whispered good-byes and how much she needed my love. The refrain begged for us to one day meet again. "Oh boy!"

Deedee started playing this song repeatedly about two weeks before going back to boarding school. She would put that darned thing on that record player, sit there, and then turn her face to me and look at me with these great big blue doe eyes brimming with tears. I thought I was going to die.

Deedee made it very difficult for me to leave her in England. I'd tell Don, "I'm going. I'm going to bring her home."

He'd say, "No, you're not. Either you're going to take the girls and go back to California, or they're going to stay in boarding school because bringing her back here's not right." So I had a choice. Either I had my husband, or I had my children. I felt that a marriage would break up if your husband was in the Middle East and you were home. I mean, what kind of life is that? And there was no safe place close by for them to receive a quality education. I felt torn.

When they were going back to St. Hilda's at the end of September, Kathy was going too. She was thrilled. I could put Kathy on a plane with Barbara and Deedee and know that everything would be all right. Ava and Bobby had been so wonderful about visiting the girls during the school year, we knew they would help us to get Kathy settled.

Ava told the story of my daughters' arrival in England as follows . . .

I remember the year when Barbara, Deedee, and Kathy came to boarding school. Don and Lorraine told us in a letter the day they were arrivin', so Bobby and I went to meet them. There was not enough time to let them know we were definitely going to be there; they just knew we would. When Bobby and I get there, out comes those little girls trotting off the plane all on their own, so independent like. I could have laughed at Don. Here was Kathy holding a check in her little hand, signed by Don. He had trusted Kathy with the check, not Barbara, not Deedee. Kathy. There was no name or amount. I thought, "My goodness, what if some crook had got ahold of it and filled in some big amount."

*We took the check. It was to buy clothes, the school uniforms, vests and underwear, shoes, and things. Lorraine sent a **big** list. First, we did the shopping, and then Bobby filled it in, and we cashed the check. Don was so trustin' natured.*

The girls had a month off at Christmas and a month off at Easter. We could not afford to fly them home for those two holidays. I wrote Sister Bridget Mary and requested the girls be together on Christmas Day. I wanted them together so they would know they were sisters and they were a family. And then the girls could be split up and go to the homes of their different school friends. Because of the lengthy stays, we offered to pay for our children to be the guests of these families. Most of the time, we got letters back from the parents saying they had enjoyed our girls and there would be no charge. I thought it was lovely of them.

When the girls came home the next summer, we went down to the Kirkuk airport to meet them. I saw Barbara and Deedee come off the plane but not Kathy. I turned to Don horrified, "Oh, my God, they've left Kathy. I don't see Kathy."

"There she is," Don pointed, "with her back to us."

"No. That girl has brown hair. Kathy is a blonde." Then the girl turned around, and she *was* my daughter. In one year, that gloomy old England had turned her pure blonde hair brown.

UNKNOWN TEMPLE, MAINLAND CHINA

Kathy never thought England was gloomy. She thrived at St. Hilda's. And her letters reflected that by being more informative and less angst-filled. She, like Mom, is a natural-born storyteller and adventurer. If you were to read those letters today, you would see that Deedee's are full of heart and drama, while Kathy's and Barbara's are quite newsy reports.

It is hard to imagine in today's world what communication was like back then.

In the late 1950s, there were no mobile phones, no internet, no email, no Twitter, no Facebook, or visual face-to-face telecommunications. Long-distance calls were very expensive and required an operator to complete — if you even lived in a place that had long-distance calling. We did not have access to placing calls to Europe in Iraq. Our options were limited to telegrams, cablegrams, and letters for overseas communication. One had to be patient, which is not easy when your child is involved. It's hard to comprehend the anxiety that such slow dispatch could engender.

The transatlantic telephone cable was laid in the 1950s, and the first telecommunications satellite was not operational until the early 1960s. Mobile phones became available to consumers in the 1980s. The World Wide Web (www) went live in 1991, and with it came the Internet providers with email and websites. Google wasn't even founded until 1998. It was the dawn of a new day when multiple forms of instant communications could take place. These can easily be taken for granted, as if such immediate exchange has always been. I can assure you, that was not the case.

The slow speed of notifications also meant that you had to have faith in the caregivers who watched over your children along the way — from hotel staff to friends to other families who took us in for the holidays, transport staff and, most importantly, the nuns at St. Hilda's. They would be the ones making those life-or-death decisions, if necessary. All required my parents to have the most extraordinary levels of trust.

The upside of this letter-writing world in which we lived is the gift of a chronicled record we don't often have today. Because of my family's letters, I have a much better understanding of the life we led. I'm also grateful to Mom's friend Margie back home, who saved Mom's correspondence for forty years and then gave Mom's letters to me. Margie knew how important they were. I treasure every yellowing fragile page of onionskin paper. Mom was a prolific letter writer, and I wish others had saved her letters as well. She wrote pages and pages to my dad when he was apart from us and to her sister in Duluth. But alas, those were lost long ago.

Please don't get me wrong, I am a big fan of today's instant communications. At the dawn of it all was the first time I used a BlackBerry. BlackBerrys had been available for only a couple of years when I purchased mine. It had no camera as those weren't available on mobile devices yet. It had voice calling with email capabilities. When I was at Paramount, I had been invited to speak at The 2nd International Forum On China Culture Industries held in Taiyuan, the capital of Shanxi province, in northwest China. Earlier that year, China had introduced an initiative to move from "Made in China" to "Created in China" and the entertainment industry was one focus of that strategy.

Then it was on to Beijing for some meetings my hosts had arranged. When I landed in Beijing, I had six hours before dinner. I arranged with a travel agency to have a car meet me at the airport and take me to the Great Wall of China and the Forbidden City before dropping me at the hotel. I hiked to the top of a section of the Great Wall and sent Roger, my husband, an email on my brand-new blue-colored BlackBerry. "I'm standing at the top of the Great Wall of China. I wish, wish, wish you were here with me." He responded before I returned to the car. I was beyond thrilled. Not having to be tethered to an office or hotel room to send an email or place a call was simply liberating.

All these thoughts about communication came flooding in when three years later I went back to China for DreamWorks. I was to represent the studio at the showroom of toy company Mattel during the Hong Kong Toys & Games Fair. Buyers from around the globe would be there, and they requested a representative to pitch the upcoming *Kung Fu Panda* movie, show footage, and hype the story.

One evening, the sky came alive with a ferocious blast and a brilliant flash. It was the beginning of what I can only describe as an epic battle between Dian Mu, the Chinese goddess of lightning, and her husband, Lei Gong, the Chinese god of thunder. Her astonishing lightning bolts split the darkness amid his relentless bellows. I watched transfixed from my sky-high hotel room as the savage battle raged on across the harbor over Hong Kong Island.

The next morning, the gods must have made peace as the sky was clear and quiet. I left my hotel, and as I did every day in Hong Kong, I ate the best gelato — ever — in an underground promenade as I trekked to the Mattel showroom. Then, on Saturday night, an unexpected fireworks extravaganza happened that rivaled any New Year's Eve display. I would have missed it if I had gone home as scheduled. There were just so many fortuitous happenings during this trip.

I observed the strangest artifact on top of the HSBC bank building, so I asked the concierge, "I think I see cannons on top of the HSBC building — is that possible? Is it some kind of city defensive weapon?"

"Oh, no, madam. The HSBC building, which was built with excellent feng shui, mounted the cannons after their rival, Bank of China, built their tower full of bad feng shui. The cannons are there to protect HSBC and deflect the evil energy back to the Bank of China." How could I not love this city!

For my Saturday explorations, I hired a car and guide from the same travel agency as before in Beijing and went all over Hong Kong Island, where Victoria Peak is, along with Jackie Chan's home, Repulse Bay, and Chun Wing's Curio Shop. I had visited the curio shop twenty years earlier when I was a buyer for the May Co. and found some lovely items there. The driver stopped at a couple of jewelry places that my mother would have loved, but baubles are not what make my eyes sparkle. After that, we went back underneath Victoria Harbor and into the countryside to visit an ancient walled city and an equally ancient temple.

At this sacred temple, I lit incense cones instead of candles. The cones are spiral rings that hang from the ceiling and burn for days in honor of a loved one. I felt compelled in that moment to light three incense cones — one for Mom, one for Dad, and one for Roger.

Hanging from the center of each cone was a card on which I could write a brief message before unfurling the cone, lighting the incense, and having the caretaker hoist each into the rafters. Although I went to boarding school later than my sisters, our letters all started the same way. What did I pen on my note to Mom before it was lifted to the heavens? Perhaps, you can guess: "Dear Mom. How are you? I am fine. How did you ever manage when we were gone? I miss being able to talk to you. I miss *you* . . . every day. Love, Pam."

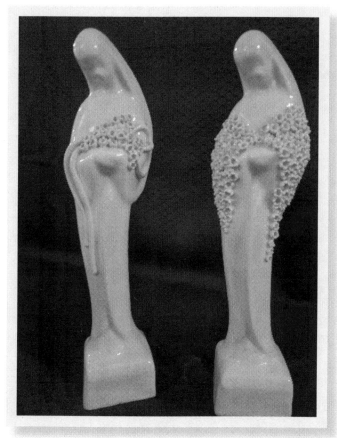

Hazelle Louther
She managed to avoid all cameras but created beautiful sculptures!

21 "She was dripping in diamonds"

LORRAINE — KIRKUK, 1959

When traveling, one talks with many people. You know how you get friendly and say, "Here's my name and address. If you're ever near my house, please come and see me." We had met several individuals during our travels that we casually invited to visit us in Kirkuk. We never expected to see anybody, of course.

Imagine our surprise when a year later, after Kathy left for boarding school, a letter arrived. "Remember me? I met you on the bus in Spain. Can I come to see you?"

What are you going to say? I wrote back and said, "Sure." Don and I racked our brains trying to figure out who this Hazelle Louther was. We couldn't even remember what she looked like!

We had no idea how she was getting into the country — how she would get her passport okayed and secure a visa. It was not that easy for foreigners to visit Iraq. By God, pretty soon we got a notice that she would be arriving the next week. I wouldn't go to the airport because I didn't want to be embarrassed when I didn't recognize her, so I sent Don. I felt he'd stand out, and Hazelle would remember him because of his height and his chiseled good looks. Before heading for the airport, Don worried, "How will I know which one she is?"

"I don't know," I replied, "but as she is coming on the company plane, she is likely to be the only woman to disembark."

In the meantime, I called my friends in camp, told them

I was expecting a visitor, and would they please help me entertain her. There wasn't much to do in camp, so I really needed their support. To also prepare, I moved Pam into the back bedroom that was adjacent to ours and gave Hazelle Pam's room.

Hazelle proved to be a charming and elegant older lady. I think she was about sixty-five at the time. She had gray hair, was beautifully dressed, and model thin. Hazelle wore high-heeled shoes with nothing but straps over the top of them. They were handmade in Hong Kong. Her clothes were all silk, and they too were handmade in Hong Kong. Of course, she had a mink stole. She was dripping in diamonds and appeared to be rolling in wealth.

Hazelle turned out to be quite clever and jumped right into the middle of things. She went out in the kitchen and made cookies. Hassan thought she was great. She would go galloping around camp, walking down by the wadi that ran past our house. On one of her treks, she collected pampas grass to adorn our living room. And she made a footstool from the five-gallon tins the Dancow powdered milk came in. Hazelle took about seven of those and bound them all together. Afterward, we went into town and bought some red corduroy. She used it to cover the tins, having added cotton padding to the top. *Et voilà*, a fluted footstool shaped like a child's drawing of a flower, curved around the edges. Besides her camp hikes and do-it-yourself projects, we went out to coffees and teas at friends' houses and to the club for dinner. My friends were so generous to help entertain.

I remember one day I went into Pam's closet (which was the room Hazelle was using) to get one of her little dresses. On the floor there was this rag thing that had straps on it. I thought, "What did Pam leave in here?" When I picked it up, it had a zipper. I opened the zipper and I almost dropped it, I'll tell you, because I was *so* shocked. The pocket was stuffed full of hundred-dollar bills. When Hazelle came back from her walk, I took her in the bedroom and said, "Look here, Hazelle, I have an honest houseboy, but what is this? I thought Pam had left something in here, but there is money in it."

"Oh, that — that's my money belt. I made it. It fits under my bra." It fit over one shoulder and tied around the other side of her bra. Apparently, she didn't believe in traveler's checks.

Her husband died before her daughter was born. I asked her why she hadn't remarried. She said she never found anybody who could support her "in the manner in which I can support myself." Hazelle seemed to be an investor of sorts, and apparently people befriended her, and she made a mint. I felt Don and I should have handed her his paycheck and said, "Invest it," in this wheat, cotton, cattle, or whatever commodity things she was in. She was ever so clever with money.

Hazelle also told Don and me some fascinating stories. She told me about how she and her daughter had been kidnapped by monks in the hills of Korea. Her daughter was one of the few interpreters of either Chinese or Japanese (I can't recall which it was) in World War II. Later, her daughter married an army major, and they had two daughters of their own, one of them named Mercedes after Mercedes-Benz. Benz's daughter was a personal friend of theirs. Hazelle told us all about the time she'd spent in the Orient and all the treasures she had collected there.

Don told our friend Peggy that Hazelle must be a member of the CIA. She might have been, but Don never voiced that to me, probably because he knew I would ask her. But Hazelle did say she had recently come from India, where she purchased some jewels for her daughter. The jewels were from a maharajah's collection. She only paid a minimum down and would not pay the rest until they delivered them to her in the United States. And she told me those jewels she was getting from the maharajah's collection were something like $250,000. I was horrified. I had never heard of such figures. And I got the distinct feeling they were to be smuggled into the U.S. What a character!

We are the only people that I know of in camp who had a visitor. I don't recall another American nor a Britisher having a guest. Not a mother or dad or aunt or uncle. Of course, the kids came out. But nobody else ever had company in Kirkuk except the Newtons. And it was a strange circumstance that we had one. I mean, Kirkuk, Iraq, wasn't exactly your typical vacation spot.

Of all the darned things, Hazelle said that she was going to go to Israel when she left Iraq. She had a friend there who was a colonel in the army. She had a visa in her passport, but I told her she couldn't get to Israel from an Arab country. She would have to go through Cyprus. She went to Beirut anyway, demanding to go to Israel. Later, Hazelle told me she ended up at the Lebanese police station, playing cards with the police captain there, but they still wouldn't let her go to Israel. Even Hazelle, with all her considerable charms and apparent connections, had to go through Cyprus to get there. We never could go to Israel even though I would have liked to have visited the country. If your passport was stamped for Israel, you never got back into an Arab country and couldn't work in one again.

When we came home in 1962, we went up to see Hazelle in Carmel. She had a little house where one had to park the car nearby and walk. Outside of it there wasn't grass or anything. Instead she had all these oriental dogs and very valuable statues. I'll never forget her sugar bowl — it was jade. She had flower arrangements made of different shades of carved jade in colors that I never knew existed. She had magnificent oriental screens that I have never seen the likes of. Her oriental collection that she had told us about in Iraq was in evidence everywhere.

In her house in Carmel, there was just a little bedroom upstairs. I slept on the couch, and Don had to go down a ladder to the basement to sleep. We retired for the night, but I was afraid to close my eyes because I was scared I might throw out my arm and knock over one of those priceless objects occupying every surface and cubbyhole in the place. Everything was gorgeous around her house. It may have been a tiny house, but it was filled with really lovely things.

On top of her considerable talents, Hazelle proved to be an accomplished sculptor. She gave us a sleek white Madonna figure and Madonna bust made from porcelain. She gave Peggy a set too. Peggy and Hazelle had also formed a bond, as Peggy supported me more than anyone else in entertaining Hazelle.

Another interesting quirk about her had to do with Christmas cards. Every year, she sent out Christmas cards the day after Thanksgiving. She would make them herself out of construction paper and pinking shears with last year's Christmas card images cut and glued on the front. It tickled Peggy and me so that Hazelle would do this. She wouldn't seal them either, choosing to tuck in the flap so each card could be mailed cut-rate. For a woman with all that money, she was kind of cheap in some very odd ways.

Every time I got a Christmas card from Hazelle, she would write, "Well, where is Don going next." I felt certain that had we ever gone anyplace out of the country, Hazelle would have shown up on our doorstep. Hazelle visited Peggy and Mann in Texas and again when they settled down in Australia, Peggy's home country. I actually think Hazelle was a professional visitor traveling from place to place to place.

ST. CARTHAGE'S CATHEDRAL, LISMORE, NEW SOUTH WALES, AUSTRALIA

In the ensuing years back in the States, we often had visitors and often were the guests ourselves. My aunt and uncle and cousins came in a camper. Sometimes the visitors were my sisters' college friends. Sometimes they were our friends from overseas and sometimes the relatives we had missed while growing up abroad. Peggy came several times as did Ava, maybe a half dozen or more. On many occasions, there were bodies sleeping on the living room floor, us younger ones having given up our bedrooms. It was a noisy, full-of-life home with conversations in all kinds of accents. Mom was not overly fussy about the state of our residence, explaining, "My friends come to visit with me, not my house." There were many warm greetings and corresponding sad good-byes.

One thing Mom wanted us to understand was how to be a good guest. We were expected to help, be tidy, make the bed or fold the blankets, do dishes, take our hosts out for a thank-you meal, express gratitude, and *never* complain. When we had visitors, it was guests first: make sure our guests had eaten all they wanted before going for seconds, ask if they needed anything and, again, *never* complain (about giving up your bedroom or seat or anything else).

I hope I have learned this lesson well. I endeavor to be a congenial guest or gracious host, feeling honored to be in a friend's home or have a friend in mine. I worry about overstaying my welcome, so I have a tendency to make my visits short. My one exception perhaps was visiting Peggy in Australia. I so enjoyed our time together that, in retrospect, I may have imposed a bit longer than she preferred. On more than one occasion, she tried to dissuade me, saying, "I'm afraid you'll be frightfully bored, my dear." But she never could. I was never bored with Peggy. My job and life in the States were so intense, Lismore was a place of solace, where I could breathe and relax. I doubt Peggy ever understood how much I loved our conversations, my sunrise walks, her amazing cooking, afternoon naps, quiet time to read, and playing games in the evenings. Ironically, as I reflect on those visits, I'm betting that Peggy likely made a few calls asking her circle if they would help her entertain me!

On this visit to see Peggy in Australia, I knew I was not going to overstay my welcome. Our head of Australasia had resigned, and I was filling in until a new person could be appointed. I had only the weekend with Peggy in Lismore before flying out on Monday to meet with our agents in Seoul, Korea. Peggy was a devout Catholic. We always went to church on Sundays at St. Carthage's. This Sunday was no different. We had laughed the night before over dinner about how she and Mom had teamed up to entertain the unanticipated but infinitely memorable Hazelle. It reminded me of how much fuller our lives were made by opening our home to the unexpected, to the traveler.

So that Sunday as I lit my candle in St. Carthage's Cathedral, I thought about how much Mom enjoyed meeting new people and how easily she made them all feel welcome. Mom was a great host. "Thanks, Mom, for a life made rich by unique and wonderful guests."

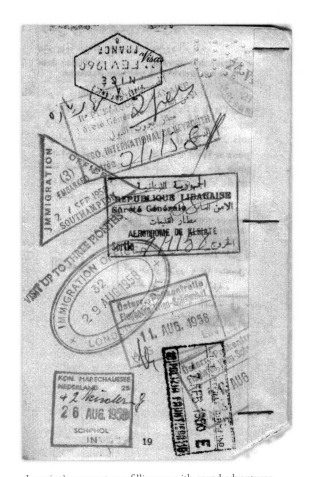

Lorraine's passport was filling up with grand adventures

LORRAINE — HOME LEAVE, 1960: CONTINENTAL EUROPE

When we came back from each of our long home leaves, I would spend the subsequent two years planning the next one — the places I wanted to see and the things I wanted to do. Don and I would argue back and forth about it, finally settling on an itinerary. In February of 1960, our second home leave was to begin in Istanbul, Turkey, continuing through Rome, Monaco, Lisbon (Portugal), and ultimately California to see our family and friends. We would return via England to spend the Easter holiday with our girls. That would be the best part by far.

When Ava and Bobby left Iraq for good right after the revolution, Ava gave me her Iraqi passport and some love letters from Bobby. She was afraid to take them with her because the customs officials were conducting intense searches of all belongings and people leaving at that time. Two years later, when we left, things had relaxed. I decided this presented a good opportunity to smuggle them out because we never knew what the future would hold.

I had an old girdle that had become slack over the years. I put it on, and I jammed it full of Bobby's love letters and Ava's Iraqi passport. We too had things I felt were important to take with us on this trip such as rolls of undeveloped film and pictures. I had a loose bra. The film canisters were distributed throughout. Then I tied a nylon stocking around my waist, filling it with other things. Lastly, I put on a baggy jacket and full skirt to hide it all. It was hot. I had to wear that jacket 150 miles down to Baghdad to catch the flight to Istanbul. By the time we got on the plane I was most uncomfortable. I said to the stewardess when we were up in the air, "Would you please tell me when we are over Turkey?"

"What in the world for?"

"Well, you know, there has been so much trouble in Iraq. I just want to know when we are over a free country."

Dutifully, she came and told me when we were over Turkey. I picked up my flight bag and went into the lavatory. I came back so much more comfortable and pounds lighter.

We stayed at the Istanbul Hilton. It was a beautiful hotel with a lobby filled with these giant poufs scattered around. We had a lovely room, high up the tower. Immediately, Pam raced out on the balcony and hung on the railing throwing her legs around looking at the city below. Terrified, I begged, "Don, grab her. Grab her."

He said, "She's all right."

"But it's high up. Grab her." I was rooted to the spot, and I couldn't move towards her. To this day, I am frightened of heights.

Pam's shoes were worn through, so the next day we went down to the bazaar to find something for her feet. The bazaar was something to see. Huge in comparison to the souk in Kirkuk town and filled with so many more things. They had a gold bazaar that was much bigger than what I had seen in Beirut, Lebanon. My eyes were popping out of my head, believe me. I had never seen anything like it. When we were in the bazaar, I spotted some red leather shoes that had little turned-up toes, Turkish shoes. I said to Don, "Well, let's get Pam a pair of those to wear until we get back to the States."

From Turkey, we went to Rome. Don had been to Rome before, but I hadn't, so he watched Pam, and I went on all the tours. Upon my return, we would feed her an early dinner so we could go out in the evening. She loved the pizza and salad. She would order a salad and a small pizza. When asked if she wanted ice cream for dessert, she'd say, "No, another salad, please." She loved salads because we didn't have lettuce in Kirkuk. When Pam would eat two salads, the waitstaff couldn't believe this little kid wanted another salad rather than ice cream.

We flew from Rome to Nice. The scenery from the cab window on the ride from Nice to Monaco was absolutely stunning. We were driving along the French Riviera, gazing at the Mediterranean Sea I so loved from one window while viewing the sculpted green mountains of the French countryside with graceful chateaus sprinkled about from the other. I don't think I closed my mouth the entire journey; it was that breathtaking.

I was very excited when we got to Monaco. I wanted to see the casino and the palace where Princess Grace lived, the cathedral where Princess Grace was wed, and, well, everything. From all my reading about the Monte Carlo casino, I learned one should wear formal attire, long evening gowns and tuxes. I went to work pressing my gown and Don's tux on towels on top of the dresser. We took Pam out for her dinner and then back to bed in the hotel for the night. Everywhere we went, we showed her how to use the telephone if she became frightened. We told the desk clerk that she was alone in the room, and we told the hall porter, who would check on her.

I dressed in my gown and Don in his tux. Don went to the desk to ask for a taxi, and the man said, "It's just a block." Naturally, we walked. It was midweek, with few people at the casino. I was shocked to see that they were not very dressed up. We had to pay extra to go into the fancy rooms like you saw in the movies. Everywhere we went, Don was mistaken for a dealer because he had on a tux. Everybody spoke French, so I only played roulette, putting my bets on the red or the black to make it easy to know if I won. All in all, it was a very disappointing evening. Not a glamorous experience like in the movies.

Our next stop was Lisbon, Portugal. We set out to see the sights and walked way up to the top of a hill to see the medieval castle São Jorge (Saint George). On our way back, we saw these markets that had great big wine vats in them. Of course, Don had to stop and see. He wanted to taste some sherry. You're supposed to bring your own bottle, which we hadn't, but they found us one. Don bought a pint of some kind of delicious liqueur that we took back to the hotel and enjoyed during our stay. We went to a restaurant for dinner that featured Portuguese dancing as the entertainment. Pammy delighted in imitating their moves. Again, we would put her to bed and notify everybody in the hotel she was alone because we wanted to go out and enjoy the evening.

Don and I went to a club with traditional Portuguese folk music called fado. The ballads sung to the accompaniment of guitars were so soulful and felt so sad. While there, we heard about a casino on the Portuguese Riviera west of Lisbon called Casino Estoril. Apparently, during World War II, spies and agents from the warring countries gathered there, as Portugal was a neutral country. It was also supposedly like Las Vegas. Well, I just had to see that! So off we went in a cab to Estoril. Don wanted to gamble. Not me — I wanted to see the floor show. I'll tell you one thing, I'd never heard the Tennessee Ernie song "Sixteen Tons" sung in Portuguese, German, French, Italian, and Spanish. Now I have. I always felt Don was stupid to simply gamble when he could have been watching this wonderful show.

Lisbon had just opened its first subway. It was so clean you wouldn't believe it. Each station was beautifully tiled. We decided to ride it to the end of the line and back, which proved a much less convoluted experience than our double-decker bus and underground adventure in London. It turned out there were numerous families enjoying the ride, many of whom picnicked as they rode from one end of the line to the other.

We descended to the platform on an escalator, a rather new device there, judging by the reaction of a Portuguese family's mama. They were trying to coax her to ride it, but she wasn't about to step on this moving staircase thing. When she finally did, she began swaying back and forth and yelling at the top of her lungs. Having boarded just ahead of her, I was scared to death that she would fall on top of me.

Lisbon was magical, truly one of my favorite cities in the world. I was sad to leave it. But leave we must. We took a plane from Lisbon to New York. I think it was an old prop job because it took us hours and hours to get there. The leather shoes I found for Pam in Turkey had already worn completely through. When we arrived in New York, it was snowing. I said, "I can't take her out with holes in her shoes." Luckily, there was a shoe store across the street, so I carried her to the shop and bought her a proper pair of shoes.

We spent a couple of days in New York, and then it was time for us to head home to California. Don's old oil-field buddy owned apartments. Bill had a furnished apartment empty, so he said, "Well, you're going to be here a month. Stay in it." Gratefully, we did. My aunt Gertie came down from Portland, Oregon for a week while we were there. We enjoyed visiting all our friends, Margie and Russ especially, and relatives, exchanging stories of the last two years.

Too soon it was time to depart again. We went back to England for a visit with our good friends Ava and Bobby. When we arrived at their flat in Welwyn Garden City, Bobby had a fit about me smuggling out Ava's Iraqi passport and his love letters to her. "They could've put you in jail, girl . . . and thrown away the key!"

To which Don said, "Yes, and I would have left her there and come on leave!"

The Easter holidays were coming up for the girls. We had

made up our minds that I would stay in England and take the girls somewhere for Easter, as Don had to get back to work in Kirkuk. We went up to see them before Don left for a couple of days.

Unfortunately, Don experienced quite an eventful return. I began a letter to Margie that took me several days to complete.

(Friday) It's 1:30 A.M. so this will just be a short note. Bob is working nights and Ava just went to bed. We've been jabbering away.

Don got away this morning. His flight was cancelled yesterday but he didn't know it until he had turned the car in and made a trip to the airport. We got the telegram here 15 min after he left. Newton's luck! He got back here at 10 P.M. last night and left again at 7:00 A.M. this morning. Hope he is on his way. And hope they don't fine him being two days late getting back. Also, I should have gone with him — he managed to lose his Iraqi work permit, resident book, pass & his notebook! Wouldn't you know. Hope they are turned in to the London police. Honestly — that man!!!!!

We had a lovely weekend with the girls. Kept them out of school Monday all day. They looked wonderful! Barb hasn't grown anymore. A size 12 would have been fine. The one I got was too big. Deedee hasn't grown a bit & her dress was 2 sizes too big! Kathy looked bigger, but everything fit. (Guess that's because Deedee stays little.)

I know you will get a kick out of this. Pam hadn't spoken for more than 5 minutes when Kathy looked at us and said, "Pam sure has a funny accent — I never noticed it before — but she sure doesn't sound like she belongs to us!" Don and I could have died 'cause the older three are so English. Pam doesn't *sound English at all. Everyone around **here** knows Pam's an American by her accent. Haha. What do you mean Pam sounds like a "limey" — you just never heard a **real** one!*

*(Monday) Didn't have a chance to finish this over the weekend — will try now. We had a card from Don this morning — he was delayed in Amsterdam. Honestly, I wonder if he made it to Kirkuk **yet**!*

I'm freezing to death in this country. Took me just 2 days to get a dilly of a cold. I'm recovering slowly, but my bones are still chilled. Brrrr! Haha. Have so much to do this week. We have to get into London one day — really need 2 days there. Have to decide when Pam and I are leaving and make arrangements. Also have to go by the I.P.C. company offices. Have to buy myself a couple more sweaters. I brought warm vests (undershirts) & am wearing them! They are saving my life. Must buy Pam a coat before she freezes to death too.

Ava thinks I'm terrible writing my friend these things when it really is lovely weather. Oh brother. It's loads of fun being with Ava and Bob again. They are such nice people. They are moving back to Scotland next month. Delayed going a month because we were coming.

PS Don forgot his electric razor at a hotel here. Hope to get it back! He went back to Iraq without one.

I needed a place to take the girls for their Easter holiday. Bobby and I pored over various publications, and he pulled out info about places that he knew. Bobby and I sent twenty letters with about a dozen replies. I ended up booking a place called Rose Cottage in Combe Martin, a picturesque coastal village in the southwest of England. I just enjoy the names of houses and towns in England — Puddletown, Rosedale

Abbey, Watermouth, Darlington, Ramsbottom, Pack O'Cards Inn, Oswaldtwistle — they make me smile. For our holiday, I was envisioning this beautiful thatched-roof cottage covered in climbing roses. Yes, a fun seaside holiday in Devon sounded perfect. I decided that's where I would take my girls.

ÉGLISE SAINTE-MARIE-MADELEINE, PARIS, FRANCE

Mom was constantly planning interesting places to go and things to do, and so was I. I can recall only one proper vacation while I worked for DreamWorks. Most of my "vacation" was a stolen day here or two days there tacked onto a business trip or a long weekend. According to my math, I made about ten trips a year, visiting from two to five cities each time. Some trips extended over two weeks to include a weekend. I did this job for over five years. All of those Saturdays and weekends added up to about eighty to ninety days of sightseeing and visiting with friends. Not just internationally — I loved visiting my cousins Ron and Luanne in Iowa. With them too it was great family time filled with lots of laughs. This was the glamour side of my job. There were other times when I just wanted to be at home, sitting in my peaceful garden with absolutely nothing to do. Or maybe have a long visit with my sister Donna, as Deedee preferred to be called as an adult, or my best friend, Elena, jabbering away, as my mom used to say.

As long as there was an opportunity to do something or go someplace, my mother's spirit egged me on. I had many conversations with hotel concierges that started with, "I only have a couple of hours. Is there something close by I can go and see?" They never failed me. Bravo! you wonderful ambassadors of your city's hidden treasures. Those amazing men and women also helped me retrieve a mobile phone left in a cab, finagle theater tickets in London, book a day tour to places like Monet's house and garden in Giverny, or tell me about a little garden or small gallery just around the corner.

Christmastime was always a treat when I was abroad. I was delighted by the holiday decorations in Paris and London. Then there were the renowned German Christmas markets. I walked around one when I visited Berlin. While there, I also toured several museums on Museum Island. Housed there are the monumental Pergamon Altar and the Ishtar Gate, which was built as an entrance to the ancient city of Babylon, located in Iraq. And of course, I had to tour the Reichstag, home to Germany's parliament along with Cold War–era points of interest, Checkpoint Charlie and the Berlin Wall remnants.

I awoke on December 6th to find a stocking filled with treats hanging on my door when I went to retrieve the newspaper. In German tradition on this day, children leave their shoes outside the door, where St. Nicholas fills them with small gifts and goodies in the night. In some places long ago, the practice of gift giving by St. Nicholas was separate from the celebration of the birth of Christ.

These many delights on that trip to Berlin were counterbalanced by an unexpected tour of Sachsenhausen concentration camp. I showed up too early for a walking tour of Berlin and chose to go with this group instead. It was drizzling and windy when we arrived. I felt cold in my wool coat and scarf. None of the prisoners had this luxury, which seemed inhumane to me. I thought this an apt day to be there. I learned much but *felt* even more — of the overwhelming degradation of the prisoners relayed in the matter-of-fact yet vividly recounted stories of our guide. She was not Jewish. She was not German. She was Australian. When I asked her why she did this work, she replied, "Because we must never forget. So it never repeats."

Returning to Berlin, I needed to take a walk to process what I had just experienced. It seems history was not done with me yet. Behind my hotel, I wandered into a giant "field" of cement oblong blocks, many much taller than me and all longer and wider than a coffin. As I ventured further into the maze, all the city noise disappeared. I was left utterly alone with only the sound of my breathing as the darkness closed in early to claim this winter day. Underground, below the blocks created as the Memorial to the Murdered Jews of Europe, was a Holocaust museum. There I listened to story after story of families and individuals that simply disappeared. I felt very heavy and inordinately tired as I trudged back to my hotel that evening.

I was gratified I had spent that day as I had. My mother taught me to seize opportunities, all types of opportunities. A chance early arrival led to insight on a subject I'd heard and thought I knew much about, but, in reality, I had little understanding of the true depths of the human devastation.

Six months later, I found myself in Paris in the summer searching for some flowers as a thank-you to an agent who had managed a particularly tough schedule of meetings. I remembered an enchanting flower market in the shadow of Église de la Madeleine. This church looked more like a Greek temple to Athena than a church dedicated to Mary Magdalene. Massive columns surrounded the rectangular church, seeming to force all manner of traffic to divert. As I came around the corner to the front of the church, coral rose bouquet in hand and appendage briefcase in tow, posters were hanging on the iron fence announcing a concert series. One would be taking place the next evening! "How cool is that?" I thought. "Mom would expect me to take advantage of this."

Friday night, I mounted the steps, looked up at the pediment sculpture of the Last Judgment, and walked through the colossal brass doors. I was in awe of being able to partake of such an evening. A black curtain provided a backdrop for the chorus and orchestra and separated them from the opulent altar behind. I sat down on a simple wooden chair with thatched seat on the center aisle, watching the other concert goers stream in and waiting for the performance to begin. I had to believe that this was the kind of place for which the music was created. My spirit soared with the majesty of each note, my heart overflowing with gratitude that I could experience such a night in such a place. The tiredness fell away, and I felt grateful to my job for bringing me here.

Afterward, I stopped at a devotional area to light a candle for my mother. It seemed she always left room in her itinerary to take advantage of places recommended on the go, such as when my parents went to Casino Estoril in Portugal. As I lit the candle, I felt grateful for all the time she spent planning our trips and all the space she left open for chance encounters. There are just those times when you see a sign on the road and decide in that moment to change course and take a different route instead. Then a whisper escaped my lips, "Thank you, Mom, for showing me how enchanting the spontaneous detour can be."

Boarding school — Hickleton Hall, Doncaster
Barbara, Lorraine, Pam, Deedee, priest, Kathy

23 "I'll be a nervous wreck by Saturday"
Second leave, part 2

LORRAINE — HOME LEAVE, 1960: ENGLAND AND EUROPE

A few days later I headed north with Pam to St. Hilda's to collect the rest of my tribe. We had to transfer trains in London to go on to Combe Martin. Sister Bridget Mary asked if I would escort two girls into London, where their parents would meet us at the station. Of course, I said yes, remembering that lots of people had been nice to my girls.

We got on that darned train, and I think we stood half the way to London. But we got there, delivered the girls safely to their parents, and we continued to Combe Martin. Now, as I said before, I had visions of a little cottage with roses going down the path in the front and climbing the chimney. When the taxi driver pulled up in front of this store in town, I was certain he had made a mistake. He pointed to a door next to the store that had a little plate on the top that said Rose Cottage. "Here you are."

"Are you sure this is Rose Cottage?" Well, by God, he got out and checked, and it was. We went up the stairs to find our apartment was on three levels. There were bedrooms on two different floors and then the kitchen and the living room on another floor. We took the adjoining bedrooms on the same floor, and all the girls and I slept in those. There was no sleeping late because in the morning, the shop down below was where you bought bacon or cheese, and every time somebody opened the door, the bell dinged.

Shopping was really a shock to me. You went to one store for your cheese and your bacon, another one for your vegetables, another one for your meat. It was altogether different than it was in the States.

We arrived shortly before the wedding of Princess Margaret, Queen Elizabeth's sister. Well, I certainly didn't want to miss that. When I talked to local people there about going to London to see it, they said, "Do you have reservations?"

"For what?"

"Well, there won't be a hotel around, and what do you expect to do with these girls? They're going to get tired." I hadn't even thought of that. Then they suggested, "Why don't you rent a telly?" I hadn't thought of that either.

Down I went to the television rental shop. I told the man what I wanted. I told him I had planned on going up to Princess Margaret's wedding. And he said, "Oh, no. it will be much too crowded." I agreed that his was the consensus with other folks I talked to and that's why I wanted a television. I told him where I was staying. He delivered it that afternoon and connected the black-and-white TV. We thoroughly enjoyed it during the rest of our stay. Television was a rare pleasure. We did not have a television in Iraq, nor did the girls at the boarding school.

It was early May when we began our holiday. I had written to my friend Margie all about our plans for the next two weeks and gave her an update on the state of the girls.

DeeDee is still not happy without us. She's convinced now she has heart trouble. She hates school so much. I'm convinced now she will never get used to being separated from us. And oh, how my heart aches for her.

Barb is fine, enjoys school and learning. But she wishes I'd move here and send them to day school.

Kathy is voted head of her form, most popular girl

and best rule keeper. She loves it and doesn't miss us.

It's funny how different they all are. They all play the piano better than I expected. They are all extremely polite and very nice little girls. They are **much** *younger-acting than children their age in America. Don was surprised at how old Sue acted when compared to his own daughter of the same age. Our girls are much more innocent.*

I'm looking forward to getting to know my daughters again this holiday.

We were so happy to be together, just the girls and me. I would cook for them, and we would walk down to the beach, but it was not warm like California. One day, we took a bus to the next town; I think it was Ilfracombe or Barnstaple. They had a country market, and we had lots of fun going all around the stalls that day.

Another day we went down to the beach and followed it along the coast. I had packed a picnic so we could stay all day. We were just fooling around in this little cove, and a man came by. "Are you leaving?" he queried.

"No, we're staying a while."

"The tide's coming in," he informed us.

"What does that mean?"

"If you're not out of here in five minutes, you're in here for the rest of the night." Boy, did we scamper. We went over the rocks, and the water came rushing up. We had to dry our shoes.

On May 6, we spent the whole day watching Princess Margaret's wedding. How exciting it was to be in England for the event, even if we weren't in London. It was the first royal wedding to be televised, and we were there to see it. Princess Margaret's dress was so elegant. She was radiant. And she had eight bridesmaids! I couldn't help but think that I had four lovely possibilities for her wedding party sitting right there in front of me. Ha-ha.

A CANDLE FOR MY MOTHER

By the end of the two weeks, Barbara being "fine" proved to be a bit of an overstatement. The day before we were to leave our lovely beachside holiday, I wrote again to Margie.

> *Today we had such a lovely day planned. Had cleaned and packed yesterday. Planned to go to the beach all day and have lunch and tea out. Woke up to our first rain. That cleared, and we started out. Barb had a headache and took an aspirin before we left. Half way to the beach she was white, and we had to come home. Barb went to bed and the day was off. I think it is just my leaving again — she keeps everything inside her. Expect a scene tomorrow from Deedee & how I dread it. She wails! Kathy keeps everything inside too — don't know what to expect there. She's an angel — probably nothing — I hope. Golly is this ever hard. I'll be a nervous wreck by Saturday!"*

Once more, I had to take the girls back to school and go through the parting. This was horrible. I think the worst thing I've ever had to do. But Don had given me a choice: either I come back to California and put the girls in school or they went to boarding school. I knew boarding school was good for them, and it was harder on me, probably, than it was on them. I hope it was, anyway.

After returning the older girls to school, Pam and I were supposed to go right back to Kirkuk. I got to thinking. Don had been to Frankfurt, Germany, and we hadn't. The revolution caused us to miss our visit to Switzerland, and I still wanted to go. I was a bit crafty, I guess, because I waited until I made the arrangements before writing to Don. The deal was, when you go to an Arab country, they pick up your passport. You can't leave the country unless your husband says you can. When I wrote him, I said I wanted to know if I was still an independent woman, because I didn't want him to control my life completely. If I was, then Pam and I were going to have a little side trip before we came back. I explained that we were going to go see Frankfurt and Geneva, Switzerland, and then we would fly home to Kirkuk. But I mailed the letter kind of sneaky-like so that he wouldn't get it before Pam and I left. That way he couldn't object. Again, in a letter to Margie, I told her about this little deception.

> *Finally wrote Don yesterday where I'm going between London and Baghdad. Had just written him my departure & arrival dates & left the in between blank. Have had such lonesome-sounding letters (guess I'm forgiven for my packing, etc.! Ha) and he didn't sound very fierce so decided to send the news on. He hasn't time to answer. I'm going to see places come hell or high water! Anyway, I have two whole years to repent!*

Off we went to Frankfurt, Germany, Pam and me. People didn't speak much English in Germany in those days. That was one of the worst countries to go to if you did not speak their language. We went down that evening on the main street to have our dinner. We got in there, and the waitress didn't speak any English, and I spoke no German. I fell back on my usual method of communication under such circumstances, hand-signal language and sound language. I pointed to the waitress and indicated it was up to her what we should eat. Pretty soon she brought us a carafe of wine. She put two glasses on the table. She poured one and gave it to me. In the other, she poured half a glass of wine and added half a glass of water for Pam. Pam was only six years old. I shook my head no, that she couldn't have that. I wanted milk. Well, she couldn't understand milk, so I said, "*Moooo.*" She understood that. I indicated to her to bring whatever to eat. I used hand language of shoveling in food with my right hand. We had a wonderful dinner that night, and Pam did get her milk.

When the check came, I just laid out some bills for her, so she took whatever money it was and handed me back the change. I took a handful of change and put it in her hand. The waitress shook her head and wagged her finger "no" at me and proceeded to take out a couple of little coins for her tip. She handed me back the rest of it. You see, there are honest people all over the world.

When we got to Geneva, Switzerland, we had fondue. It was lovely. The hotel we were at provided a continental breakfast delivered to your room each morning. It included beautiful croissants and sweet butter. I ordered a hot chocolate for Pam and a coffee for me. Well, I'll tell you, my coffee was lousy. But her hot chocolate was so good, and the butter and the croissants were wonderful. The next morning, the order was changed to two hot chocolates.

We'd sit on the balcony of our hotel having our breakfast and look up at the Swiss Alps. I told her, "There's where Heidi lives."

Excitedly, she asked me, "Oh, can we please go and visit Heidi?" I think *Heidi* was all my daughters' favorite book. I don't know how many times I read that book aloud; maybe four or five times. But I didn't have the expertise to get us up in the mountains, and she didn't quite understand that Heidi wasn't real.

Instead, we went around the city, and we saw that there was a circus in the town under a regular big-top tent. I went up to the ticket place to try to get a couple of tickets for us. Well, they couldn't understand me, and I couldn't understand them, and I got frustrated. I hailed a taxi and went back to where we were staying. I was telling the concierge at the hotel how disappointed I was. There was a circus in town, and I wanted to take my daughter to see it, but I couldn't make them understand I wanted to buy tickets. He said, "Would you like to go tonight?"

"Oh, yes, I would, very much."

"Not to worry, Mrs. Newton. I'll get you tickets." He immediately picked up the phone. He secured tickets, and he ordered a taxi to take us there and bring us back to the hotel. All we had to do was go to the ticket window and pick them up. To avoid any difficulties in collecting our tickets, the concierge wrote me a note in German. We had excellent seats on the aisle right where the clowns entered the ring. One of them pinched Pam's toe. She laughed so hard. She was so cute and so vivacious. Everybody around was pointing at her and laughing along with her. She loved those clowns.

Intermission came along, and the tent started to empty. I said, "Come on, Pam, let's go see where they're going." Well, they joined a line. So we joined the line. We didn't know what the line was for. When we got to the front, servers were placing sausages in pieces of bread and the people were ordering either a beer or a soft drink to go with it. So we had the sausage in the bread and a soft drink too.

Of course, everything was in German. We couldn't understand a thing. It didn't matter. We thoroughly enjoyed that circus. It was a wonderful evening. I remember it to this day. I hope Pam does. As promised, the taxi was waiting for us when the performance ended, returning us to the hotel safe and sound.

I've never been sorry that Pam and I had that little trip to Germany and Switzerland before we went back to Iraq. Whatever penance I would have to do, it would be worth it.

ST. PETER'S CHURCH, EATON SQUARE, BELGRAVIA, LONDON, ENGLAND

Mom wondered if I remember the Geneva circus and the clowns. I do. I also remember looking out at the Swiss Alps, desperate for Mom to take me to visit Heidi. And I remember the hot chocolate. All these memories and now every month I was making more.

I spent a marvelous Saturday in London that started out with room service breakfast. I don't know what it is, but I just love room service breakfast. Another of my favorite things to do in London is the Buckingham Palace tour. The hotel concierge secured me a ticket upon my arrival. Luckily, every year there is an industry trade show called Brand Licensing Europe, which I attended. It is where companies involved in the licensing business meet up. It just so happened that if I left on Friday night, I could make it for the last day of the Buckingham Palace tour. (Oh, and just to set the record straight, I always paid the cost of my extra night at the hotel, food, and any other expenses that were not work-related.)

Buckingham Palace has been open to the public only since 1993. In 1992, there was a devastating fire at Windsor Castle, and to manage the costly repairs, Queen Elizabeth allowed tours of Buckingham Palace in August and September, when she was at her summer residence in Scotland, Balmoral Castle. I heard there was talk of the queen stopping the tours after the repairs at Windsor were completed, but the outcry was so great, it remains open. Over half a million people visit yearly, and I am delighted to have been one of them on several occasions.

Each year the tour has a different theme, so there is always something new to see. One year, the ballroom was set up for a state banquet; another, the process of knighthood was detailed; another showed the official dresses of the queen; and yet another, the toys of the royals. The queen has the most amazing dollhouse, by the way. Probably my favorite tour was the wedding of Prince William and Catherine Middleton (2011). A copy of their wedding cake, her shoes, acorn-and-oak-leaf teardrop earrings given to her by her parents, the queen's Cartier tiara, and of course that fabulous wedding dress were all there.

Some random occurrences have happened on my travels but none more surprising than this one on the wedding tour. You proceeded through several rooms in the palace before you entered the actual display area. At the start of the wedding display, there was a video about the making of the wedding dress. I was sitting enthralled, watching for the second time, finding the detail truly awe-inspiring. My friend Samantha moved away to look over at the displays we were to encounter shortly. While I sat engrossed in the video, a query came to Sam across the dividing banister by a young woman. "You seem to know her," she said to Sam, pointing at me. "I think that's my mother's cousin. Is her name Pam Newton?" Sam affirmed it was and motioned me over. I was blown away. What are the chances of meeting my cousin Sharon's daughter Jenny halfway around the world? This took place at the only spot in the tour where it doubles back on itself, and Jenny, who had met me only a couple of times in her life, recognized me. It was a happy chance.

On another visit, I went on the Buckingham Palace tour by myself as my London pals were busy. The tour ends on the terrace (veranda) at the back of the palace, where a large tent is set up. There one can sit, have a snack, and look out over the queen's private garden. I chose a cup of tea, a scone (another fave), and a chocolate sweet. While I enjoyed my treats, I texted back and forth with my best friend in California. I joked that the queen had stood me up for tea… yet again.

I wandered out of the gardens, through the handy souvenir shop, where I loaded up on gifts like Buckingham Palace jams, Advent calendars, lace cookies, royal mugs, and crested tea towels. I continued past the lake to the street behind, Grosvenor Place. To my right was Wellington Arch and Green Park, where my hotel was located. Deciding not to return just yet, I set off walking and exploring. I was soon lost as London streets are not all straight lines but more often than not, curve and wind their way around. Even though it was getting late, I wasn't worried. After all, I could always hop in a cab if I really couldn't find my way out of this maze. It seems I'd wandered into a bit of a residential area. I came around a corner to face Eaton Square, one of the many private gated gardens so prevalent in London. There stood a church, St. Peter's, still open this late afternoon.

I went in. I suppose I felt a little melancholy, having spent the whole day by myself. I was tired, the tea and scone snack on the terrace had worn off, my hands hurt from carrying my packages, and my family and friends were so far away. Thoughts of boarding school drifted in, which quickly turned to thoughts on how difficult separation from family is, especially for a child from the parents and a parent from a child.

Most people that I know in America don't send their children to boarding school, but my parents had little choice. The effects of losing her brood one by one took a toll on my mother. Mom worried that we were terribly unhappy being separated from her, especially Deedee. But by the time we left to relocate back to the States, Deedee had learned to enjoy being at St. Hilda's, even expressing a desire to become a nun. I asked her recently if she hated boarding school. She responded, a bit surprised, "No. Why? Not at all."

During our final year overseas, I would join my sisters at boarding school and without my sisters there with me, especially Deedee, I do think I would have died of a broken heart. It was hard for me, but I can't help but think how much harder it was for Mom. Children are resilient. I survived, which gave me the ability to cope much better with separation and loss as an adult.

Now, as I reflected in the simple elegance of St. Peter's Church, boarding school took the form of being a very enriching experience, as my mom had hoped it would be. I told Mom what I hadn't said to her in life: It was all okay. I thanked her for the experience, acknowledging I was all the better for it.

Crazy hat contest

24 "There's no way I can send that one on her own"

LORRAINE — ENGLAND, 1961

Summer came and once again we were a family. Everyone was throwing parties. Everyone was at the pool swimming. Everything was fun. We had all our kids home, and we were happy.

But in September, Pam was going away to boarding school. I could send Kathy alone, but I couldn't send Pam. I just knew she would get up in that airplane and decide, "I want to go home." Then she'd open the cabin door and jump.

I told Don, "I have to take her to boarding school. There's no way I can send that one on her own." He understood. We made the arrangements, and I took Pam to England.

By this time, there were so many restrictions on our movements and activities in Iraq. The Iraqi government still wouldn't allow pictures to be taken out of the country. We couldn't take any pictures of a woman nor any of a man. I had pictures of Hassan. I had pictures of women on the street. I had my Damon watercolor prints of everyday Arab life painted in Tehran that I prized. I decided to package up three footlockers, and I told Don, "I'm taking them out of here now. I'll stash them in England until we go on leave next year." I checked with my British friends about storage options, and they told me where to call. A friend of Don's happened to be on the customs desk at the airport when Pam and I went through. He didn't open any of the luggage. I escaped with three footlockers full of the things I most treasured.

At the Grosvenor House hotel in London, I called the storage places that people had recommended. The prices were horribly high. I found myself once again at a concierge desk, asking the gentleman if he had any suggestions. He did, replying, "Well, madam, just leave that here with me."

"But I won't be back for a year or eighteen months."

"Not to worry. I'll take care of it for you. I'll put it in our storage room here."

"How much?" I inquired.

"No charge."

Well, when I got back to Kirkuk and told Don, he almost had a stroke. "Oh, you've just lost it all," he predicted.

"No. I don't think so," I replied. (My instinct proved to be correct. The footlockers were there when we returned to claim them.)

After our footlockers found a home, it was time to return my girls, all four of them this time, to boarding school. Sister Bridget Mary made arrangements for me to stay at a woman's house close by. I sat there sewing on these damn labels for days. All Pam's clothing and accessories required labels. Every item had to have one. Every sock, every pair of pants, every everything.

Again, I wrote to Margie.

> I came to England September 19th to put Pammy in school with her sisters for the first time. What a mad rush my first week here was! We stayed in London shopping for three days. The school has moved to Slights, Nr. Whitby in Yorkshire (Northern England) due to the death of Lord Halifax on whose estate the previous school was located. The schools are beautiful and clean. Everyone so nice. The countryside the loveliest I have ever seen. The younger girls are at a place called Woodland Hills. Barb's at Carr Hall about 2 miles from Woodland Hills. Both

are St. Hilda's Schools. They will see each other every week. Woodland Hills is a self-governing school and the day I left, Deedee had been voted "Head Girl" by her fellow students and Kathy appointed "School Leader" by the nuns. These are the two most important posts in the school & they were so proud.

*Still have to go to London again for a couple of days shopping. Also, must do the girls' Xmas shopping and wrap it. **That** will kill me.*

Things are still unsettled in Iraq. Still censors too! The Kurds were up in arms fighting the army when I left. The oil talks not settled. We are down to about 8 American men in Kirkuk and 3 wives. About 200 British. There used to be over 600. We never know from day to day if we have a job. Smuggled out all my films this time . . . along with my albums, linens, embroidery, and all the girls' clothes for our next leave.

Once Pam was established at the school, I went down to stay with my friend Sheila from Kirkuk. She was on leave in Shoreham, not too far from Brighton, in the very south of England. I stayed with Sheila a month because I didn't know if Pam would walk out of that school or run away or what, and I wanted to be within calling distance.

The girls knew to write me there for the first couple of weeks. The first letter I get from Pam said, "Dear Mummy. How come I don't have a teddy? Everybody here has a teddy."

I called Sister Bridget Mary and asked, "What's a teddy?" Well, it was a teddy bear. The next day I took the bus into town to buy her a teddy bear. I bought a much smaller one than I should have, I'm sure. She still has it to this day. But I didn't know everybody had a teddy in England. Kathy had never asked for one.

While I was at Sheila's, Pam seemed to have settled in, so it was time to return home. On my way back to Kirkuk,

I stopped in Basrah. It is at the southern tip of Iraq and the country's main port and shipping terminus. I had never seen Basrah. It is where Don worked when he first went to the Middle East, and I wanted to see it. I visited with friends for a couple of days before I went home.

Home to Kirkuk was the saddest thing I ever did. I didn't have any children. I was so unhappy, you couldn't believe it. They called me from the club and asked me to handle the Christmas party because I had done it in the years before. I said, "I can't. I really can't. There's no way I can do this without my own children here."

I remember Christmas Eve so clearly. Don and I went to the Church of England services with Sheila, who had returned from Shoreham, and her husband, Ian. After the services, we went home, and I locked myself in one of the girls' bedrooms. I cried all night. I didn't have my kids. I was so unhappy I thought I was going to die.

ACTON HILL CHURCH, ACTON, GREATER LONDON, ENGLAND

My mother clearly missed us all. Over and over again she recounts the hardship of being separated from us. Her job besides wife was mother. Now she had no children to mother, and being a wife was not a full-time job. Dad was often gone for days at a time, working on drilling rigs far from camp. Hassan was in danger as an Iranian in Iraq illegally. The company was not the fun place it was before. Many of her friends were gone. Every day was a worry. Internal fighting continued, and the Iraqi government was taking a harsher stance with IPC. Things were disintegrating around her.

Mom wrote in a letter to Margie this line: "Did I tell you Don is working in Ain Zalah oil fields? If not — call Phyllis Bowen — wrote her about my secret fears the other day."

Ain Zalah is a little over forty miles, or seventy kilometers, northwest of Mosul in the heart of Kurdish territory, not far from the Turkish border. Mom's words haunt me. I wish I had read that sentence before she died. I would have very much liked to ask her what her secret fears were — she appeared so fearless to me. I do know these were challenging times.

In an email to an old friend, who also traveled heavily for his job, I wrote about my challenges at DreamWorks.

> Gosh I have been crazy busy in this job. I am in week number three of a three-week tour of Europe. I was in Paris for week 1. In London for week 2. Spent this past weekend visiting Ava in Scotland. Back to London Sunday night for more meetings and then it is on to Germany Tuesday night. I will be home on the 7th of October and back in the office on the 8th. But you know better than anyone about being on the road so much.
>
> I feel so out of touch as I have been working the kind of hours I promised myself I would never work again. It's a great company. The job / my boss runs me ragged though. I really need a bit of a break.

My break would come at Christmas, when the studio closed for a week and all my sisters and I were together. It meant a great deal, as it was the only time in the year the four of us were in the same place at the same time. I was to be the host.

At the beginning of December, my boss wanted me to arrange a London trip. "No retailer will want to see me now. This is their busiest time," I argued without success. The result was me getting caught in the "Great London Snowstorm" of December 19th, when Heathrow was shut down and newspaper headlines decried "Not our finest hour" about the treatment of the stranded passengers.

Waiting to board the plane, my fellow passengers and I watched with apprehension as the snow fell, getting heavier and heavier. Boarding went off without a hitch. Then the captain's announcements started — "They are plowing the runway." "The de-icing truck will be here shortly." — as we watched the snow pile up on the wings and ground around the plane. We were hopeful, though, as we could see an occasional flight taking off. After three hours, the flight was canceled. The crew would exceed their flight time if we left at that point because this was a direct flight to Los Angeles. We deplaned and went to collect our luggage. There were no accommodations at the airport.

The studio's travel department found a Double Tree Inn in Ealing Common, where I could stay until they found a way to get me home. It was not that far, several stops on the Piccadilly line to Acton and then one stop on the District line to Ealing Common — or twenty minutes by car. The problem was, almost nothing was moving. The underground had massive delays, and taxis could not be found. Thousands were stranded. After several hours, I made it to the underground station near my hotel. It was eerily quiet. No cars were about. No shops were open. Only a silent winter scene as I slogged from the station with my big suitcase, rolling briefcase, and all the Christmas duty-free items I'd purchased in a new satchel slung across my shoulder.

The next morning, I bundled up and went exploring. Had I complained I needed a break? Well, I was getting one. Playtime! The result? A snowman in the park across the road, a snowball fight with a tree (I won), and a poem called "A Winter's Walk in Ealing Common." The poem was inspired by a house with a front porch filled with snow-mounded terracotta crocks of varying sizes, which I reimagined as the village of the Flower Pot people. Impossible to see in my normal hurried life

Continuing my walk, I rounded a bend to see a church, Acton Hill Church. I knew it was a long shot, but I mounted the stairs to try the door. It was locked. As I walked away, the faintest sounds of music emanated from the church's tiny gated garden, drawing me in. There I found a meeting hall, windows glowing with golden light. Inside, a choir was singing Christmas music. I didn't feel comfortable just walking in, so I brushed the snow from a wooden bench and sat for a while.

I was alone and thinking about my mom and that first Christmas spent without her girls. Mom always said she wanted a big family.

We would have been six kids if Dad had agreed. She loved being a wife and mother. Her family was her world. It must have been so hard for Dad too. How did he console her? I would be sad indeed if I couldn't get back to California soon. Being alone without my sisters at Christmas was unimaginable. In that moment, I felt Mom's sadness. It is so painful to think of her crying. If I could light a candle right now, I would tell her how much I wished I could take away her tears — the tears she cried when her mother died, the tears she cried when my father died, and the tears she cried leaving us in boarding school. But she taught me tears are a part of life. The important thing is what you do after the tears. I wish this was one lesson I didn't need to learn and one gratitude I didn't need to give.

Parents visit in Slights on their way back to the U.S.A.
Barbara, Deedee, Kathy, Pam

(25) "The writing was kind of on the wall"

LORRAINE — KIRKUK, 1962

All the girls were away at boarding school in England, and now it looked like the last member of our family would leave Don and me too. The police were looking for a Persian houseboy in Baba West, the area of the camp where we lived. We managed to get the orders torn up — but it was not safe for Hassan to stay. He was going to try to make it home to Iran. We had talked about it and figured that the time was probably coming for him to return. He said he was going to marry a policeman's daughter. "Big strong woman," he said. Hassan was all of about 5'5", 130 pounds soaking wet, and he thought he was about twenty-one. Of course, he didn't know his exact age, but if he was correct, it would mean Hassan had been working for us since he was sixteen.

In our years together, I would tell him, "Now, if you have chikos, you feed them orange juice. And if you get a mud hut, plant a tree. It'll be cooler in the summer and warmer in the winter. Plant a couple of trees around your mud hut." I also instructed him to "feed his chikos milk and good things." He knew about powdered milk. He used to mix it up from those five-gallon Dancow tins for the girls. We kept it in the refrigerator and got it real cold so the girls would think it was real milk, although we never really fooled them.

During all the years he worked for us, Hassan had not taken his pay. He wanted us to save it for him. It amounted to a lot of money, hundreds of dinars. For Hassan to get to Iran, he had to walk maybe 150 miles or so. His hometown was right over the border from Iraqi Kurdistan. It was very dangerous. There were bandits on the roads. He would not be safe.

I was afraid that someone would kill him for all that money. Once again, I took the jacket he was going to wear. I took the shoulder pads apart and put some money in each one. Then I cut open the sleeve lining and put some money in the lining. I put money around the waistband of his pants. I sewed money into each cuff. I told him to put his spending money in each sock in case they took his shoes. I felt, if they got his money, maybe they wouldn't get it all, only a part. When all was ready, he slipped away with our love and gratitude into the silent desert.

I never knew the route he was taking or heard if he got there all right. I pray he made it. I decided not to hire another servant. I'd never find another Hassan. Also, I felt I should "break in" again to *work*. It had been a lovely, restful, weight-gaining five-plus years. I knew I'd never have it so easy again.

By this time, the writing was kind of on the wall for all of us. Things had been heating up between the Iraqi government and IPC. Everybody that went away for leave didn't return. I remember Peggy and me packing up a couple of houses because the family hadn't bothered, thinking they were coming back.

When it came time for us to go on our next leave, Don and I argued. I told Don, "We're not coming back."

He believed, "We are."

I didn't believe, not me. "No way." So I ran a sale, and I sold off everything.

I sold off the washing machine. I'll never forget the guy that came to buy that. I had my price, and he said, "I have so many chikos. I need this and for so much less."

I said, "I have four chikos. I can't give it to you for less." One person I remember buying a cake decorating set. I wonder what this Arab gentleman ever did with that because he didn't know what the heck he was buying. But he only paid about 70 cents for it.

I sold everything. Don still claimed, "We're coming back."

I said, "I don't think so." I packed up everything in case we didn't come back because when the Neeses left, they didn't come back. Mann Nees only had nine months to go for his pension. Don had eighteen months to go for his pension. I just knew that we were not going to make it. And we didn't.

Even so, I had been planning our leave as I always did. I wanted to go to California via the East this time. I wanted to see the Road to Mandalay, like in the song. Don put his foot down. "No way. We've got to go through England and see the girls."

It's not that I didn't want to see the girls. Of course, I did. But they would only be four months behind us if we were shipped home as I expected. I thought we would be seeing plenty of the girls from then on. This adventure could be our last, so I wanted to go. Don refused. I never did get to see the Road to Mandalay, and I didn't visit India and China and Japan, all the things I had planned.

February 1962 rolled around, and it was time for us to go on our leave. We flew from Baghdad direct to London and of course went straight up to see the girls. When we got there, it was so dang cold you wouldn't believe it. And snow. They had a railroad station hotel just down the hill from the school, where we decided to stay. I asked if we could have the girls come and stay with us, so they did. It was miserably cold. I asked the stationmaster's wife if she would put these tubes of hot water in the bottom of the bed to warm it up. I was freezing to death. I said to Don, "You take two girls, and I'll take two." I took Deedee and Pam to my bed. I just wanted two warm bodies on either side of me.

The next day, we all went out for tea at this charming restaurant. Of course, the girls were all excited. Their parents were there. It was Mummy this and Daddy that. My daughters had complete British accents by this time. There was an English couple sitting at the next table who couldn't help but overhear our conversation. After a bit, the lady leaned over to me. "Oh, you are such a nice American couple adopting those four little British girls."

"No, no, these are all mine."

"Oh, but you and your husband are obviously Americans, and these children are British. It's lovely of you to adopt them."

"Madam, if I adopted them all, I would have mixed up the sex a little bit." I don't think that woman believed me to this day.

After our visit, we went to see Ava and Bobby in Scotland. They had adopted a cute little girl, and they named her Lorraine after me. I was so thrilled.

We continued to California. There we were informed we were not to return to Iraq. When I knew for sure, I wanted Don to go to Libya. Saudi Arabia. Iran. Somewhere. I didn't care. I said, "I'll go to England, and I'll put the girls in day school, and then when the older ones graduate from St. Hilda's, I'll take them to Switzerland and put them in finishing school as day students traveling between there and London." I didn't want to come home. But Don did. I wanted to keep this big adventure going.

THE POTTER'S WHEEL CHURCH, MBABANE, SWAZILAND

Why did my mom stay in Iraq all of those years under such unpredictable conditions? I believe my parents felt if trouble really arrived at their door, they could escape its wrath. Call it hubris or call it naïveté, they never felt that they were in life-threatening danger. The working conditions were good at IPC, the camp life was still enjoyable, and Mom wanted Dad to earn the pension he had been working so hard to achieve. But it was not to be.

Mom was just thirty-nine when our family returned to the United States. She clearly wanted more adventures and would get a couple later when my dad was working in Kuwait, although she never made it to Asia. Once all of us girls were in American schools — one in grade school, one in junior high, and two in high school — it was much more challenging to manage a life overseas with the family in tow. Dad lost his pension with IPC but continued to work in foreign assignments while Mom kept the home fires burning. It was hard on them to be separated eleven months of the year with Dad home just one month at a time. But we were to stay in California regardless of where Dad worked. They felt it was important for us to have some stability as we entered our teenage years. They wanted us to graduate from American high schools so we could go on to American colleges. My sisters and I would make our future here.

Years later in that future they helped build for me, I was consumed with the Sainsbury's *Kung Fu Panda* concert in the park at Althorp for many months. I was so excited by this project. It had never been done before, and it was thrilling to be first and working with such an amazing set of partners, especially Paul at Sainsbury's and Hans Zimmer, head of DreamWorks Studio's film music division and head of his own film score company. I'll never forget Hans rehearsing the orchestra in the rain on the estate the night before the event. We had a dinner right out of *Downton Abbey* in the Spencer dining room. Althorp House is also where most everyone stayed.

The morning broke with a light drizzle that the sun quickly dispatched. Rain was our biggest worry as this was an outdoor affair. We had been sweating the ticket sales in the weeks leading up to the event. The sheep field beside the house had been transformed. There were Chinese acrobats, kung fu demonstrations, giant kites, and kids' activities galore. The chairman of Sainsbury's helicoptered in to Althorp with the Chinese ambassador. Hans Zimmer conducted a two-hour concert of music and songs from DreamWorks films. I considered this a highlight of my career, so much so that I asked Donna to come to London to experience it with me. In the end, 12,500 people came to enjoy what is called in England a family day out.

I don't think any of us working on this project in either the U.S. or the U.K. had taken a day off almost from inception. When it was over, I took two days and then came back to work. A day later, my boss called me in. I thought she might be giving me a week off to get caught up on my life. Instead she told me DreamWorks was closing the London office, and I would now be managing EMEA (Europe, Middle East, and Africa). In reality, the EMEA business was focused in Europe, so logistically that would be feasible. But the workload, wow. There would not be enough hours in the day. I felt this was a recipe for failure — my failure.

It seems the writing was now on the wall for me as well. At some point in the last number of months, something happened. The environment at work turned from crazy busy to stressed-out toxic for me. I realized I was just not happy, and I was just not happy for far too many days in a row. Europe was fairly quiet in August, but come September, the race was on. I had to make my decision by September, and it would be very difficult. Not only did I love the company, my job, and so many of my colleagues, but I had worked hard for a bonus that I would lose if I left before the end of the year. I thought of my dad losing his pension when he left Iraq. But this would be my choice and not the result of government action. I felt I had a little more control over my life, at least. I took a month to sort through my finances, talk with my sisters, and create a plan. In September, I gave two months' notice. When I reflect on my time at DreamWorks now, it can be a blur until I slow the frames down and see all the funny, heartfelt, crazy times I enjoyed.

Life may be a bit uncertain at times, but I never doubted there were amazing adventures still to be found. I took my frequent flyer miles and booked a trip around the world. I wanted to go back to Swaziland, where I had gone after my husband, Roger, died. It was a healing experience then, and I believed it would be again. On that first trip to Swaziland, I met a retired nurse, Bonnie, who was so touched by the plight of the children there that she began a charity. At seventy-two! I had been supporting her charity and wanted to chronicle her work. I brought a fancy camera with high hopes. I think I needed a bit more cinematic training as the footage did not nearly reflect her work and her passion.

First stop on my around-the-world tour was London to see my friends and Ava in Scotland. Then on to Swaziland. And finally, a visit with Peggy in Australia. I returned home just before Christmas. Part of me wanted to see if I could find the Pammy of my mom's stories again. And if I could, I was going to write that book about my mom I had started so many times in the years before. I felt incredibly optimistic about my future endeavors and still do.

I was in Swaziland for six weeks, and it was honestly one of the best experiences of my life. Bonnie and I drove all over the country to accomplish her charity work, and giving back restored my soul. We went to a couple of different churches, but one in particular, the Potter's Wheel, was especially welcoming. I sat there to reflect on my mother. I was grateful for so many things. The lessons she taught me have proved invaluable. But I think these stories she spent hours recording are among her most priceless gifts.

Not only am I thankful Mom preserved our history, but I am grateful to have glimpsed Lorraine, a fully formed, multidimensional, complex woman that I will love and miss until the day I die. This day, my appreciation was for her. There is no one else I have ever wanted as my mother and my friend. "Thank you for teaching me to believe in possibilities and to reach for the stars. Mom, I am grateful for you. I will never stop lighting candles to honor you."

About the Author

Pamela Newton is a veteran marketing executive with over twenty-five years in the entertainment industry at Paramount Pictures and DreamWorks Animation. Infected at an early age by her mother's adventurous spirit and love of worldwide travel, Newton grew up to embrace a similar lifestyle, grateful for any and all opportunities to travel the globe. Currently, Newton divides her time between writing, traveling, and teaching.

You are invited to visit the author / book website www.PamelaLNewton.com, where you will find lots more information. You can hear Lorraine's voice as she tells a story, see additional pictures, and read Pam's blog.

Please feel free to contact Pam via email at Hello@PamelaLNewton.com.

Made in the USA
San Bernardino, CA
08 May 2018